EMBRACE YOUR WEIRD

Also by Felicia Day

You're Never Weird on the Internet (Almost)

EMBRACE YOUR WEIRD

Face Your Fears and
Unleash Creativity

Felicia Day

GALLERY BOOKS

NEW YORK LONDON TORONTO SYDNEY NEW DELHI

G

Gallery Books
An Imprint of Simon & Schuster, Inc.
1230 Avenue of the Americas
New York, NY 10020

First Gallery Books trade paperback edition October 2019

GALLERY BOOKS and colophon are registered trademarks of Simon & Schuster, Inc.

For information about special discounts for bulk purchases, please contact Simon & Schuster Special Sales at 1-866-506-1949 or business@simonandschuster.com.

The Simon & Schuster Speakers Bureau can bring authors to your live event. For more information or to book an event, contact the Simon & Schuster Speakers Bureau at 1-866-248-3049 or visit our website at www.simonspeakers.com.

Interior design by Faceout Studio

Manufactured in the United States of America

10 9 8 7 6 5 4 3

Library of Congress Cataloging-in-Publication Data

Names: Day, Felicia, 1979– author.
Title: Embrace your weird : a guided journal for facing your fears and unleashing creativity / Felicia Day.
Description: New York : Gallery Books, 2019.
Identifiers: LCCN 2019025239 (print) | LCCN 2019025240 (ebook) | ISBN 9781982113223 (paperback) | ISBN 9781982115746 (ebook)
Subjects: LCSH: Creative ability. | Creative ability--Problems, exercises, etc.
Classification: LCC BF408 .D39 2019 (print) | LCC BF408 (ebook) | DDC 158.1/6--dc23
LC record available at https://lccn.loc.gov/2019025239
LC ebook record available at https://lccn.loc.gov/2019025240

ISBN 978-1-9821-1322-3
ISBN 978-1-9821-1574-6 (ebook)

To Calliope catbird.
I love you just the way you are.

CONTENTS

INTRODUCTION

I've been plagued with anxiety my whole life. It wasn't until I started creating that I finally felt free enough to show off my weird-self. I want to help you show off your weird-self too.

A few years ago I wrote a memoir called *You're Never Weird on the Internet (Almost)*. It was a *New York Times* bestseller, which made my mom really proud. She even got out of a fender-bender situation right after it came out by dropping my name. "I'm Felicia Day's mom!" she said to the person she'd just rear-ended. Luckily, the victim had read my book and was mildly impressed, so they let my mother off scot-free without calling the insurance company. (By the way, I heard this story from the fan, not my mother. Anyway!)

Since I wrote that book, I've heard over and over again how my story helped some people not feel so alone about mental health issues, especially anxiety. And how that book made it possible for others to overcome their fears and start creating things! What kind of things? Well, I've heard from people who were inspired to:

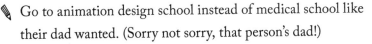 Start a nonprofit ferret rescue group.

Go to animation design school instead of medical school like their dad wanted. (Sorry not sorry, that person's dad!)

✎ Draw a web comic about smart-ass bees.

✎ Build a custom Batmobile. Fully driveable!

✎ Write a fantasy trilogy, which they completed in the time I wrote HALF a book, so I got intimidated and asked for THEIR autograph at my own book signing. (It was awkward.)

✎ Form a steampunk band that was NOT named Clockblockers but hey, it's a good name, go ahead and take it.

✎ Name their hedgehog after me. (I end with this because it's probably the coolest. Have fun eating carrots, Felicia Bae!)

In short, "I made X because of you!" became the most gratifying thing I'd ever heard. And I realized that expressing our weirdness is a baked-in superpower we all have, but for some reason, many are afraid of using it! Life is so much easier when we conform and stay silent, right? Easier, but one of the greatest disservices we can do to ourselves. Aside from wearing high-waisted pants. (Seriously, they don't look good on anyone. *I will fight you over this!*)

Helping other people accept their weirdness and use it to create is something I've become super passionate about. It's top three behind playing video games and eating high-quality croissants. I now consider it one of my missions in life to give people a power-up to overcome destructive voices that keep their creativity silent. It's personal. Because I've been plagued by similar voices all my life.

Destructive thoughts kept me afraid to pursue writing for many years—and discouraged me when I finally tried. I thought they were "realistic." That those voices knew better. It was an amazing feeling to realize one day, "HEY, HERE'S A CRAZY IDEA! I DON'T ACTU-ALLY HAVE TO BELIEVE THESE THOUGHTS! IN FACT, THEY CAN SUCK IT!"

When I finally made an effort to work on my issues, I started making things. In fact, I found a career through creating. *Who'da thought?*

Aside from (over)sharing a lot of my opinions, I have filled this book with exercises designed to uncover the joy of creativity. To help people beat back the fear that keeps them from trying new things. And to inspire everyone to embrace how truly awesome and unique they are. (Yes, I'm pointing to you with these words. Imagine my 3-D holographic finger sticking straight up out of this page. If I accidentally poked anyone's eye out, sorry!)

Most of the exercises in this book are joyful. Some are silly. Some dive into the ugly. But all are designed to help uncork the creative voice. They're techniques I've cobbled together over the years from therapy, motivational posters, and trying to answer the simple, desperate question, "I want to say things. Why can't I be brave enough *to just say them?*"

We don't need lofty goals going into this process. I'm not here to guilt anyone into upending their life and becoming a professional macramé artist or something. (Although if you do, I'm excited for you and would like to order a plant holder.) If the only thing anyone takes away from this experience is "Gosh, I forgot how much I liked to sing heavy metal tunes in the shower!" that's okay! Rock on, fellow cool person! I'll sing show tunes in support!

Simply put, this book is about uncovering, unblocking, and letting loose FEELING. And then activating ways to SHARE THAT FEELING. ←-ƒ That is the most basic description of a creative urge I can think of.

ACTIVATE [FEELING];
INTERPRET [FEELING];
SHARE [FEELING]...
CREATION COMPLETE

Ready?! Let's hold hands and skip down creativity lane together! Or not. We don't have to hold hands, it's cool. Let's go!

oxox

Felicia

HOW TO USE
THIS BOOK

Obviously the goal is to turn the pages and read and write.
But I want to offer advice on how to approach
the work so you can get the most out of this experience.
(Or I'm just a control freak and can't
stop micromanaging. Either/or.)

I hate throwing parties. It's just ahead of GOING to parties on my top-ten "least favorite weekend activity" list. (Other items include bikini waxing, doing my taxes, getting my car serviced, and cleaning out the fridge. Okay, I'll finish the list: awkward family brunches, visiting theme parks, bra shopping, and taking stock of where my life is headed before crying myself to sleep.) When I'm in charge of a party, I take the responsibility way too seriously. I hyper-curate my invite list so there won't be too many people. But later I panic because there might not be enough, so then I invite more, praying that everyone WON'T actually come but hoping that 75 to 80 percent do. Actually, 73 percent works Baby Bear perfect. THEN I get super worried that there won't be enough food. So I get double the snacks and triple the number of drinks. I order so much food that I'm basically eating leftover veggie platters for the rest of the month. When people don't show up precisely at the start time, I get crushed and log on to Instagram, convinced I'll see my feed filled with other parties my friends are attending instead of mine. And finally, when people DO show up, I flit from person to person with the speed of a caffeinated hummingbird, desperate to provide each person with the perfect party experience while not giving them a chance to experience any time with me whatsoever.

No wonder my last house party was in 2005.

ANYWAY that neurosis is why I wanted to start this journey off with some best practices of using this book. I'll be here the whole time, sharing my very awkward personal experiences along the way, but this journey is about YOU, dear reader. (Ripped that off Jane Austen, you're welcome!) By the end we all want to walk away feeling empowered and enthusiastic about getting our voices out in the world. If that doesn't happen, well, no one gets their money back, so I guess use this as a doorstop or something. Let's get started!

Work Fast/Think Less

Try to work without censorship. I would say consider everything done here a "vomit" draft, but puke is *probably* an uninspiring visual for most people. Our goal is to uncover our unique creative identities. So write quickly! Work like an important part of you is buried in an avalanche and needs air, STAT!

If you notice you have a tendency to overthink with pen in hand, try answering a question out loud, like you're talking to a friend. Or doodle pictures instead of using words. Whatever form of expression is more fun, work THAT way. "Fast and fun" is the laxative that will help relieve our creative constipation. (Another grotesque visual. You're welcome AGAIN!)

_— _— _— _ _ — _— _— _ _ — _— _ — _

Try it on this page. You just opened the front door and a dinosaur in a tuxedo lunges for your face! *What do you do?* Fill up the page with what comes to mind! Incomplete sentences or drawings are fine. Just *GO GO GO.* You have five minutes! Put a timer on and start!

Ding! IT'S DONE NOW!
That felt good, right? Are you tempted to read back over what you did? DON'T DO IT! What you did was PERFECT! Let it goooooooo!

_— _— _— _ _ — _— _— _ _ — _— _ — _

No-Judgment Zone

We don't have to LIKE anything we do here. We don't have to be remarkable. We don't need to dazzle anyone. C students welcome! It is so easy to forget that we have every right to create something *even if it's not "good"*! Guess what?

It's our human right to be crappy at something and still enjoy it! Yes I'm using Comic Sans. Because even though it's the butt of every typography joke, I still enjoy its whimsicality!

I will be honest and say that drawing and other visual arts aren't my strong suit. As a kid I would gift people with paintings at Christmas, and the polite response of "You tried so hard, honey!" was the standard reaction. But when I'm feeling stressed, to this day, I will start doodling and the "AUGH!" of it all seems to disappear with every crooked cat face and malformed vanishing point I dump on the page. The process works for me. All those deformed kitty faces? Meaningless.

So every time an exercise makes you freeze up or locks you in your head, dive in and deliberately do something terrible. Do the worst work possible. It's okay to suck here! In fact, it's encouraged.

— — — — — — — — — — — — — — — — —

Draw the WORST picture of a horse in the space below. Make efforts to draw as badly as you can. Overachievers uninvited!

That sucks! You nailed it!

— — — — — — — — — — — — — — — — —

This book is designed to uncrack what we haven't been able to get out of ourselves. The us-as-self-critic can come later—AFTER THIS BOOK.

In an ideal world, we're able to feel confident and passionate about everything we do—especially our mistakes.

Free Up Your Pen

Breaking rules is part of creating. So consider nothing sacred. Including this book. Doodle everywhere! *Do it now!* We're taught not to damage books, but screw that preschool teacher's voice in our heads! I give everyone permission to damage the heck out of this one! Take that, Miss Julie! Start by crossing out this very sentence.

Did that feel naughty? In a GOOD way? Goooooooooood. Keep that feeling going. FILL THIS WHOLE BOOK WITH YOUR BAD BEHAVIOR! I give everyone permission to trash my heartfelt work. It's okay! I'm not in your house watching. That would be creepy.

If something I write in here doesn't sit well, cross it out! Write a retort! Rip out pages and hang them on a bathroom mirror to see first thing in the morning. Think something's stupid? Tell the book!

I'D RATHER NOT BE RUDE, THANKS.

Remember, this book is the format, but WE are the playground!

— — —— — —— — —— — — —— — —

Vandalize the heck out of this page! Markers, pens, glitter, whatever. Graffiti your heart out.

Then tear it out of this book. Yes! TEAR. THIS. BOOK!

— — —— — —— — —— — —— — —

Be Fearless

To get through all the layers of resistance we've built up over the years, we'll need to do things that might feel uncomfortable or wrong. (Ahem, only ON PAPER.) Yes, there will be "touchy-feely" stuff that may cause eye rolls. I get it. I roll my eyes when my dad sends me birthday cards that say "World's Favorite Daughter." But overcome inner groans of embarrassment and do the work anyway! What's the worst that could happen? We all become crystal-toting hippies who do hug piles at nighttime? Doesn't sound bad to me!

Actually, let's take the gloves off now.

— — — — — — — — — — — — — — — — — — — —

Write "I am the greatest thing since Swiss cheese," over and over again below.

Now let's go one step further: take a moment to risk believing it.

REALLY believe it. Picture yourself as the literal *greatest thing invented since Swiss cheese!* And keep writing it!

See? No one showed up to mock us. The confidence police didn't roll up with their sirens on to remind us of messing up at work last week, or how our thighs are a wee bit too big for our jeans. Feelings of self-worth, however grandiose, are safe here. (And whether we believe it or not, we ARE the best thing since Swiss cheese. Parmesan? Well . . . that's debatable.)

Feelings Are Our Friends

No one molds a sculpture, invents a recipe, or designs a new building with the impulse of "Meh." Emotions are the basis of all creativity. And resistance. So if a strong emotion comes up while working through this book, positive or negative, GO FURTHER INTO IT! "Gee, why do I NOT think I'm the greatest thing since Swiss cheese? Is it lactose intolerance? Who taught me NOT to be proud of who I am, and how can I punch them?"

It will help not to rush through the book. Treat the ideas here like a dense chocolate flourless cake that you have to nibble and savor because if you dump it inside you all at once, it will feel like a thousand-pound brick in your stomach. After each section, take a bit of time to think about how the ideas in it apply to you, especially with regard to your emotions. Something make you angry? Notice it. Excited? Notice that too! (If you're ever bored, that's my fault and I'm sad about it, but don't worry, that's not your problem.)

In the process of cleaning out, we may find things that are delightful. (Like a twenty-dollar bill in a pair of old jeans. JOY!) Things we didn't know were there. (Whose pen is this? Did I accidentally steal it from someone? EMBARRASSMENT!) And things we don't want to be reminded of. (Old-boyfriend underwear. COLD SWEATS!) *All* of these things will be worth acknowledging. The more ruthless we can be in identifying what makes us FEEL, the better for our creativity.

Throw things you feel strongly about onto the fire.
Positive or negative. What makes you scared? Excited? Anxious?
Words, phrases, ideas, write or draw whatever comes to mind on the
fire below! Write so much that the whole area becomes black.

If we feel a big emotion around it, I promise we can use it to fuel our creativity!

Protect Yourself

Try to keep the process of working through this book private. I know this is kind of a bizarre request in an oversharing world, akin to "Felicia told me I can't talk for a month and can only eat lima beans and need to move to a commune in the Azores now," but it's only 272 pages long! You will survive! The goal here is to unearth what's been hidden inside of us, that's afraid to be seen. Having other people's eyes on us just invites self-consciousness. Think about it: ketchup smudges on our faces aren't that big a deal unless someone else sees them, right?

_ _ _ _ _ _ _ _ _ _ _ _ _ _ _ _ _ _

Write five adjectives for how you feel when dancing alone.

Now write five adjectives for how you feel when you dance and people are watching.

_ _ _ _ _ _ _ _ _ _ _ _ _ _ _ _ _

Those two lists are DIFFERENT, right? Which list has more joy in it? Let's live out that one together! (And if your preferred list is the one where people watch you, congrats! I'll be supporting you, but from a deep, dark, neurotic corner.)

I also encourage everyone to scale back on using social media while working on their creativity. I know it's hard (I just tabbed over to Facebook three times while writing this page) but it will be worth it. Yes, you have permission to check it a few times a day, I'm not a monster, but then LOG OFF. And every time you feel the urge to waste time online, do a little work here instead—even if it's just scribbling "I wish I was scrolling through Twitter instead of this crap" over and over again in the margins.

Protect the process. Protect the inner creator. This space is ONLY FOR YOU!

Flow

And finally, draw a line, continuous on every square inch of this and
the next page.

— — — — — — — — — — — — — —

Throw away the idea that you will walk away from this book
with a THING to SHOW people.
You are trying to enjoy the creative PROCESS.
No goals, no pressure.
A calm, creative state of mind.
Imbued with the joy of concentration.
Creating a dilation of time.
Draw everywhere on THIS page.
And THAT one.

Fill every bit of empty space.
Sharp corners, curves, doodles,
wherever FEELING takes us. Just . . .
don't put down the pen!

KEEP **DRAWING.**
Draw over words. Draw to the edges.
There is no wrong here.

Did you notice time passing?
Or did the task eat it up?
IF SO, GOOD! WE DID IT!
THIS is the feeling of creation!
There is no "wasted time" when entering
the zone of our own minds.
*Our **unique** minds.*
And repeat silently, now and forever when creating:

I have a RIGHT to spend my time this way!

— — — —   — — — — —   — — — — —

WHY CREATIVITY

I don't mean to put anyone on the spot,
but do you REALLY know why you're here? Or did
you wander in assuming I'm funny and hope
for the best? (If so, <*insert joke*>!)

— — — — — — — — — — — — — — —

Write ten words below describing how you feel about "creativity."

Chances are some negative words come up. That's okay! In fact,
it's great! That gives us something to work on! We can't have a
makeover montage if we already look Instagram-filter perfect.

— — — — — — — — — — — — — —

Having something to work toward is motivating and makes us
feel "together." We want to be fit. We want to be more organized.
We want to learn five languages, play one thousand video games, and
visit every bakery in the world to sample every single delicious dessert. (Oops, that's my list. And now that I think about it, the bakery
thing conflicts with the whole "fit" thing, dammit.)

For most things in our lives, we depend on other people to hold our feet to the fire. First with grades in school, then with deadlines at work. We send the IDEA of our long-term goals out in the world loose and vague, like the consistency of whipped-cream frosting rather than firm, sculpted fondant. (The bakery thing is bleeding over, sorry.) The problem is, there's no way to make ourselves follow through unless we make the reasons for doing something specific and actionable and IMPORTANT. So let's specifically action up this important creativity thing, STAT!

We are here to unlock our weird, creative voices. And that means allowing everyone to be a little bit selfish in making this a life priority. *Yes, I'm giving us permission to be a little bit selfish!* I know it's drummed into us that being selfish is a terrible character trait and that's why I have to divide up my tater tots with my toddler daughter even though I REALLY want them all for myself. But there's a big difference between prioritizing our nutritional need for fried potatoes and hoarding them because screw babies, they can just eat slop. (Here are all my tater tots, I love you.)

The truth is that freeing ourselves up to create is a form of self-care. We NEED to do it. So we can be our best and happiest selves. We need to feel that truth deep in our bones in order to get started. How? Well, to start . . .

Our Voices Are Unique

Write about a cat below. A cat you know personally or just make one up! Describe the way it looks and acts, its likes and dislikes.

True story: no one else has ever described a cat exactly the way you just described a cat. *Never in history. Never again.* Isn't that amazing? We are genetically programmed to describe cats completely differently from each other! Why would evolution bring us here? (Unless the universe is run by cats. Hmm . . .)

WE WILL DISDAIN YOU BUT YOU WILL LOVE US ANYWAY.

If I were to read someone else's story about a hero standing on the beach bare-headed, mushing sand in their toes, about to jump in the ocean, I would definitely think . . . *YUCK! Why aren't they wearing sunscreen? Don't they know about melanoma? And why are we on the beach? Sand is awful. Also, the ocean is not a bathtub. It's cold and full of dolphin pee. Why would someone put a hero* **THERE** *when they could have just as much fun inside with air-conditioning? This theoretical story sounds more like how I would introduce a supervillain. I'd title the book* Twisted Beach. ⟵🗲 Totally normal thoughts.

But the cool part is that maybe reading that story could make me change my mind about beaches. Or maybe sharing my own viewpoint on that story could persuade others that sand is, indeed, horrible. (Better outcome.) In short, everything that happens, happens because SOMEONE shared their creativity first. What a beautiful reason to raise our voices! (Also now you know why I've never walked on the beach in Los Angeles even though I've lived here for more than fifteen years.)

At the heart of it, being creative allows us to understand ourselves better. Just like fingerprints or personalized music playlists, our creativity couldn't come from anyone else. The world *deserves* to hear our voice during our time here on this earth. Not to guilt-trip anyone (okay, it's a little bit of a guilt trip), but by not creating, we are robbing the world of our unique point of view. Why hold out like that, friendo?

We're Already Doing It

When I hear people say, "I'm not creative!" I get really frustrated and want to hug them tight and whisper in their ear, "Please rethink that. I know you could create something beautiful if you'd just allow yourself to try. I bet you've already done five creative things today that you don't appreciate and if I had the time I'd sit down and we could figure it out together. But this hug is getting way too long. I need to let go now."

We are creative EVERY DAY. Creativity isn't just about painting a Picasso (only Picasso could do that), it's about the way we uniquely navigate our day-to-day worlds. The way we put an outfit together. Where we pick to go on vacation. What we choose to put on our tacos. (I love ranch dressing on chicken fajitas AND I'M NOT ASHAMED OF IT!) Every small impression of "ME!" that we exert on the world around us requires a dollop of creativity. It's unconscious. And wondrous. And super unappreciated. Why?

"Weird! Odd! Bizarre! Eccentric! Quirky! Strange!" As I see my toddler daughter grow up and start to become familiar with the world around her, I notice that she focuses on aberrations. They fascinate her. She points out that a car doesn't have a roof. Wonders why one bunny in a book has a top hat and others don't. She wants to know why Mama has so many pictures of herself around the house, and when I explain that it isn't about my face, people made those pictures for me and I appreciate their art, and that most people don't really do this (and probably shouldn't), she nods and goes back to playing with Legos. She isn't pointing these things out like the differences are bad (unless I indicate they are, like french fries found on the sidewalk are NOT a good snack), she's just constantly trying to understand how the world works.

As we get older, though, that open-hearted fascination with things that are different somehow morphs into disdain. And that's when labels of "oddball" and "weird" start to be slapped on people. To set them apart. This is tough to stand up against. No one wants to be singled out. Just imagine going to a magic show and having the magician pick you from the audience to go on stage. Terrifying, right? Living nightmare. Someone get me a drink just thinking about it. In the face of this pressure, no wonder we shy away from acknowledging how different we are from each other! It's so much safer to pretend we're part of the herd! Moo moo, amiright?

But when we allow ourselves to appreciate all the unique ways we do things just by EXISTING, we can more readily accept the fact that, yes, we are all inherently creative. Ergo, we can be confident in our ability to create anything. Ipso facto, we already have what we need inside to achieve any creative dream, big or small! Carpe diem and stuff!

In the top square below, write a way you were creative yesterday but didn't appreciate it at the time as BEING creative.
Nothing is too small to acknowledge!
Then, in the bottom square, name a huge creative project you'd like to tackle but haven't been brave enough to try yet.

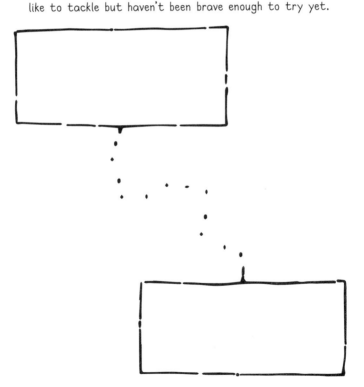

No matter how far away they seem from each other,
it's possible to connect the dots between those two things!
Just do it! Go back and draw the line!
You just did it! *SEE?*
(Of course it's not ACTUALLY that simple.
But no matter what, it *IS* possible!)

— — — — — — — — — — — — — — — — —

Together, we will learn to build a bridge between what is easy to do with our creativity and what seems out of reach. Stretch it like taffy! Or used chewing gum or . . . er, moving on.

Think Differently

We've established that no one else has the same inventory in their brain, with the exact same pathways that process the inventory, that we do. We are a special, one-of-a-kind flower—check. So it follows that shuffling our unique inventory into new, weird combos will make our brain even more complicated and weird, right? That's a good thing! I mean, the opposite of that is "simple and common." If anyone wants that . . . well, wrong book, dude. (Go look for *Average! Impose Repression and Lock Up Your Creativity!* It's definitely in the bargain bin.)

Being creative is a magical tool for growing ourselves as people. Yes, we will grow no matter what we do, that's a by-product of existing, but isn't it more exciting to CHOOSE how we grow? As opposed to allowing others to clip and form us to their preferences, like a sad little bonsai tree? We'll never know exactly what we're capable of unless we push ourselves and TRY IT ALL. Every permutation. Every connection. Shake out all the "Aha!" and "Who'da thunk!" we can get out of ourselves.

Creativity helps us combine the inventory we already have in our brains in new and interesting ways. Which, in turn, adds to our inventory. It's a free, self-perpetuating system! In a way, we're our own personal Frankensteins. (Don't go overboard and turn evil with the newfound power, please! I don't want to be responsible for creating supervillains.)

— — — — — — — — — — — — — — — —

There are two columns of words and symbols below.
Draw lines between one on each side until all are paired.

PEN	MANATEES
FRUIT	TOENAILS
MONOPOLY	PURE
FEET	1,000,000,000
LUXURIOUS	REPREHENSIBLE
4	GIFT CARD
SCREWDRIVER	GENEROUS
MAGICAL	BLEEP-BLOOP-BLOP
TWIX	FOUNTAIN
COOL	BICKER
%	NANOSECOND
TREES	THE LETTER Z
UNICORN	HYPERSPACE
BRISKET	ANNUL
CHRISTMAS	WHY?
NOT SO FAST	ANSWER
ROTTEN	FUNFETTI
MAGNETS	DYNAMIC DINOSAURS!

Now pick a pair and write/draw/create anything
at all combining the ideas on a separate piece of paper!

TAKE THIS IN: What you just wrote literally rewired
your brain in a small way. Amazing, *right?* (And a little
bit scary if you combined *Magical* and *Toenails.*)

— — — — — — — — — — — — — — —

My experience of adding up gaming + filmmaking led me to create *The Guild*, an online web show that transformed my life and steered my career in ways I could never have dreamed. Those two interests weren't unique to me. But I connected T0 these subjects in my own unique way, and then I connected them T0GETHER in my own unique way. And that combination excited me so much that I felt compelled to share it with the world. Another person's "gaming + filmmaking" would be totally different. Probably with fewer fart jokes. Who knows?

In no way am I guaranteeing anyone the mildish fame and mildish fortune I've obtained by sharing my creativity. But I WILL guarantee that if we all forge ahead in combining new things in our brains and expressing those new combinations, we will surprise ourselves with how much we can grow and reshape our day-to-day lives for the ~~better~~ weirder.

Live More in the Present

Mentally, we often fall into the trap of not being where we truly ARE. We brood over the past. We're consumed with anxiety for the future. Our brains ruminate over areas of our existence that we have N0 POWER T0 CHANGE and ignore where we are *right now*! Baller technique for increasing misery, right?

The best way to give ourselves some helpful now-gravity is to dive in and create something. *Anything.* As big as writing a novel, as small as taking a Post-it Note and doodling our signature on it for forty-five minutes. Creativity forces us to put one mental foot in front of the other. And in the end, no matter what the result, we have a THING to show for it! We may abandon that thing or throw it out in the end (like any warped piece of pottery I've attempted to make over the years), but we are able to regain our focus. And, for a moment, we're able to s t r e t c h   t i m e in a semi-magical way.

— — — — — —— — — — — — — — — — —

Set a timer for ten minutes. Then look up at the first thing you see in front of you and describe it. In the minutest of minute detail. If you get bored, start making things up about the object. What it could be used for. What it looks like on the inside. If you could sculpt it like clay, what you could turn it into. Write and write and write until the timer finishes.

DING! Now take a moment and think about those ten minutes, which would have happened whether you were creating or not. Did you notice time passing? Did it at least seem like a more enjoyable amount of time than, say, the same amount of time spent waiting at the DMV? This is what actively living in the present does for us!

— — — — — — — — — — — — — — — —

In a weirdly wonderful way, creativity slows down time. Which is, arguably, the best superpower to have. (People who want to fly? Have at it. I'll be on the ground living it up while you try to avoid bugs splatting on your face.)

Our personal timelines have a set beginning and end. All we can do is squeeze out as much in between those two points as possible. I'm greedy. I want all the life I can get. And when we allow ourselves to dig into the present with the aid of creativity . . . well, I believe it's the closest to time travel we can get.

It's Fulfilling Work

On first impression, the subhead doesn't really sell itself, right? Wah, work isn't fun! It's much more seductive to think of creativity as this untapped genius lurking inside all of us—hanging out, strumming a guitar to fill time until we finally are able to drill a hole and . . .

Our muses could then SPRING FORTH, brandishing our brilliance at the world! We could then create great things AUTOMATICALLY because the talent was inside us ALL ALONG, MOM!

<Insert cold water splash.>

Stop. All of that was super irritating. Now, hear me out about this work thing, 'kay?

A lot of what holds many of us back from creating is thinking that if we're not instantly good at something, we are not "talented." And if we're not talented, we should abandon the effort. "Try the next hill! There might be oil/gold/magic mushrooms there instead!" This is the mythology around creativity we have to dismantle. Because that's what it is. A Big. Fat. Myth.

We are all constantly "in progress." We cannot fix upon the idea that we are born a certain way and merely have to uncover our "talents" to reap rewards. We have infinitely more control than that! WE drive the car. Our interests and talents are just the vehicles. Yugo, Mercedes, van with airbrushed tiger art on the side, whatever we have to work with, get in and turn the key! Because sorry, everything rewarding in life requires effort.

This was difficult for me to wrap my head around when I was yearning to write but couldn't integrate the WORK of it into my mindset. I would start a first draft of something and get stuck in the mud by anxiety: "I don't know what comes next!" Spend months procrastinating, then end up abandoning the project because, clearly, the story wasn't supposed to be told if I didn't have all the answers automatically. In short, I didn't think I was talented because writing didn't come easy.

But no one accomplishes anything creative without effort. Yes, even geniuses have to screw their thumbs down to get work done. Albert Einstein or Kobe Bryant or Jane Austen may have had a genetic leg up at the start, but no one's masterpiece comes without effort. (Most of the greats also had the advantage of no social media. You KNOW Jane Austen would have been a Twitter addict too, right? I'm being defensive, aren't I?)

Whatever our aspirations are around creativity, whether to become a professional filmmaker or to learn how to paint happy little trees during retirement, when we integrate the WORK of creativity into our lives, we are choosing to fill our time with something that yields infinite long-term satisfaction and rewards.

— — — — — — — — — — — — — — — — —

Spend a few hours consuming another person's creativity.
(Yes, I'm making you play video games or watch TV.
Terrible homework, right?) What did you pick? How did you feel afterward?

Now, on another night, spend a few hours working on
your own creative activities. Sewing, cooking, sculpting,
writing—pick one and devote your evening to it.
Which night felt like more of an accomplishment?
Which allowed you to sleep better afterward?

Our inner creator *wants* to create. It just needs permission to do so.

— — — — — — — — — — — — — — — — —

For me, a small hat I've knitted or a cake I've baked or a comic I've written gives me infinitely more pleasure than any award I've ever gotten. And that ability to enrich myself in small ways or large helps me ride the erratic waves of external praise. It allows me to value my own existence outside of other people's opinions. And gives me a sense of control in a frequently out-of-control world.

No, I don't think creativity is a cure-all.

But I do believe it could be a cure-most.

A lot of books on creativity dive into areas of spirituality. We won't do that here. Well . . . just let me scratch the itch a bit and then we can move on.

I have an amorphous sense that we all have something more within us than just meat. An élan vital, so to speak. (In the dictionary, that's "life essence." I just wanted to include it in the book because it sounded fancy. If I ever make a skin cream, you can guess the name of it.) So just for a second, imagine that creativity is a way of giving our souls a voice. If we give no other consideration to the concept of "spirituality," just try to imagine that we actually HAVE spirits and we need to treat them nicely. They are delicate. And easily bruised. And they wither when they're made mute. Creativity gives our spirit a voice. What do we LOSE by letting it speak?

— — — — — — — — — — — — — — — — —

Now that we've talked about all the reasons WHY you should open yourself up to creativity, write in the space below the biggest reason why you're excited to embrace creativity. Be as honest as you can.

Awesome. Whatever you wrote . . .

— — — — — — — — — — — — — — — — —

YOU SHOWED UP!

I'M GLAD YOU'RE HERE!

WHERE IS THE BATHROOM?

I NEED TO SPARKLE!

OUR HERO-SELVES

Creativity is driven by our need to SHOW OURSELVES.
Weirdness and all. But first we have to answer:
"Um, what exactly do I have to SHOW?"

Apart from filling out personality quizzes in lady magazines, writing bios for work, or making an online dating profile (HURL), it's rare that we actually let ourselves stop and think, "Who the heck am I?" We're too busy reacting to what life throws at us to do stupid soul-searching.

There are too many things to consume!
Too many comments to read!
Too many parties to go to!
SQUIRREL!

Gazing inward seems self-indulgent, like for people who go on yoga retreats. Instead, we adopt labels other people give us, like "smart" or "funny," not really questioning if they're right for us or not. Sure, it's easier to exist that way, letting other people do all the us-work. But if we want to be creators, we have to know the truth of ourselves FOR ourselves. We don't have to abandon our outer She-Ras, but we have to know who our authentic Adoras are inside. (That's She-Ra's true identity, FYI. She-Ra was like Superman to Adora's Clark Kent, got it? Okay, moving on.)

My journey of uncovering my own Hero-Self has been a long and very stumbling one. When I was a kid, I gravitated toward anything that could tell me who I should be and how I should act. People said I looked like Audrey Hepburn, so I tried to walk like her, slightly pigeon-toed. It seemed to impress people when I did math, so I carried around books like *Visualizing the Fourth Dimension*. (For the record, the book was cool, but I couldn't visualize anything. I finally gave up and read all the nurse-themed Harlequin books my grandma hid in the corner of her laundry room instead.) I was so eager to grow up "right" that I forced an identity on myself rather than letting one develop in its own awkward way. "Oh no. *Marie Claire* August 2001 says people in my birth month tend to be impatient. Better sign up for that Zen meditation class, stat!"

It wasn't until I was WAY into adulthood that I started reflecting on WHY I did the things I did. Because I started wanting to know where I was actually going in life, rather than driftwooding my way through it. By asking myself hard-hitting questions like, "Do I REALLY love raw oysters, or do I just want to look fancy when throwing my head back to eat them?" I was able to reformulate a more honest sense of myself.

Bit by bit I kept digging, and that self-excavation helped fill my inner hollow chocolate bunny-self with an awareness that finally felt true to who I was. "Actually, I hate meditating! I love fairy sculptures and shopping for stationery on Friday nights at Staples! I am ME!" Over time, I started to feel like I was whole inside. And that led to a feeling of confidence that "I DO have something to say to the world, and I would love to figure out how to share it! Using this bitchin' stationery I bought last Friday night!"

In this section, we'll do that same kind of digging together. Directing our eyes inward, through the lenses of our past, present, and future, to define our creative Hero-Selves. There's nothing more wonderful than treating ourselves as homework. Self-knowledge is our primary creative superpower!

As we move through the exercises, we'll constantly be taking stock of our weirdnesses. What exactly is unique about the way we see the world? How can we identify new creative areas we are drawn to? What is our skin tone REALLY? Summer, fall, winter, or spring? (This is a reference to a '90s skin tone thing where everyone's complexion was categorized as a season so that . . . why am I going out of my way to explain this joke?)

It may help to imagine that we're all born as a map covered in fog. (Video game people will TOTALLY get this analogy.) Our life's task is to explore our self-maps until we uncover the areas where we feel most creative. Through the process of exploring our own inner worlds we will discover unknown edges of ourselves, stumble upon unexpected things we spark to, and be able to home in on where we want to concentrate our time and passion.

In short, we are the jungle, baby! Let's go exploring!

Childhood

Let's rewind all the way to the beginning. "Once upon a time, there was a little sperm named . . ." Okay, maybe not that far. (Also it's creepy to think about individual sperm having names, sorry!) When we're children, creativity is as simple as breathing. We're filled with joy when we make things. No self-consciousness. No second-guessing. We express ourselves simply because we're excited and can't wait to share the feeling.

Recently my baby made up a game. "I am a cat, Mama! You are a walrus!" For some reason this involved throwing a dodge-ball at my head and giggling a lot. We played it for an hour. Great game. Five stars. I noticed that she never questioned the logic of it. Or the quality. She had a joyful idea and needed to deploy it into the world. (And a dodgeball at my head.) I was envious. Then I googled how to roar like a walrus because I try to be a good mom.

This kind of invention is beautifully automatic when we are children. Ideas come to us a mile a minute. Everything's fresh. Everything's exciting. "Been there, seen it" is a foreign concept. *Because children have* NOT *been there and have* NOT *seen it!* We're ignorant as heck! And it's a beautiful thing! Our worlds are marvelous playgrounds of novelty that spur constant creativity! Everything is filled with discovery! Ideas spill out uncontrollably! We are fountains of spontaneous brilliance and . . .

Then we grow up.

SCREEEEEECH. *<tire skid marks>*

Pretty sure if my adult friends came over and I proposed a game of "Animal Dodgeball Head Bonk," I'd get some REALLY weird reactions. Why? Because the game doesn't "make sense." (Also we could get head injuries by throwing too hard as adults, but let's set that aside for a moment.)

As we grow up, we're constantly figuring out how the world works. Children have to learn literally EVERYTHING from scratch. Like the fact that horses don't speak human. Gravity makes things fall. Pants go on legs unless there's a dance party happening. We construct mental walls around the way we see the world out of necessity. I mean, it's probably not safe to walk around at age thirty-five thinking we might be able to fly. But the problems start when our mental walls solidify so much that ideas that fall outside them are ignored. Because, irony, it's when we're able to gaze outside those walls that we're able to come up with our most creative ideas! So how can we fix this messed-up inner architecture?

Well, we can start with some renovations! But instead of going straight into demolition mode (which sounds a bit violent when it comes to brains), let's do excavation work first. Like archaeologists with teeny-tiny brushes, we want to sweep for buried memories. Because it's through exploring how we used to see the world that we can best start to reassemble a more creative self.

— — — — — — — — — — — — — — — — —

Think of something you believed to be true as a child that was impossible.
Now pretend the impossible is possible, just for a second!
Santa, unicorns, a dream about being an astronaut, etc. It is real.
How could the impossible change your life NOW?

The best lesson we can take from our childhoods is that there
never need to be walls when it comes to our imaginations.

— — — — — — — — — — — — — — — — —

Browse through photos of when you were younger.
Pick four different ages and write them below the dolls.
Inside each of these dolls, write adjectives that describe you at
that age. Really put yourself in the shoes of a "past you."
Which of these adjectives still apply to you today?
Of the ones that have fallen away, which do you want back?

REMINDER: Every age you've ever been is STILL INSIDE YOU! Have faith that nothing has been lost. We are all nesting dolls of every age we used to be—and we can access all of them if we try!

Use an online map to locate all the houses you lived in as a kid. Then use street view to look at pictures of them. Take each one in. "Walk" around the neighborhood. Do any memories arise from these pictures? Scribble them below.

— — — — —   — — — — —   — — — — —

Name a fictional character you admired as a kid. Why did you admire them?

What about their lives did you want to experience for yourself?

Watch/read/enjoy a piece of entertainment with this character in it now. Does it make you feel closer to who you used to be?

— — — — —   — — — — —   — — — — —

LIGHTNING ROUND!

Best birthday?

Best friend?

Favorite pet?

Favorite food?

First toy?

Most hated cartoon villain?

Most awesome vacation?

Worst injury?

Snack I ate the most of when my parents weren't looking?

Posters I had hanging in my room?

Things I hid from my parents?

Ways I used to annoy my siblings/friends?

How people in school saw me?

One word that summarized my life during the years of:

0–5:

6–10:

11–15:

16–20:

— — — — — — — — — — — — — — — — —

Even if we can't remember tons of details from our childhoods, rest assured we all have ENOUGH to work with. Can we automatically remember what we got for Christmas when we were thirteen? Probably not. (To be honest, I can't remember ANY of my Christmas presents. Sorry, Mom!) But then a random memory might bubble up about a trip we took to a pancake house when we were four, or we'll be hit with the way our new puppy smelled when we brought her home when we were eight, or recall the texture of a sweater in college that we forgot in English 101 class. (It's CRAZY how it just disappeared like that. Who stole it, and *how do I get them arrested?*)

All these "involuntary memories" show us exactly how much our unconscious brains retain—they're pretty much hoarders. And the great part is that every time we dive into our pasts, it's like swimming to the bottom of a pool and bringing back up little puzzle pieces of ourselves that have gone missing. Rest assured everything we need to rebuild our Hero-Selves is down there, partying with all the pens and hair ties we can never find when we need them!

Our strongest childhood memories tend to center around emotions. Shock. Joy. Mortification. More mortification. The incidents were jarring enough for our brain to put them into long-term memory, rather than dumping them like the average day of "Played with the dog. Watched TV. Had pizza for dinner. Epic Saturday!"

While I was writing my memoir, I took the time to list the strongest memories from my past I could think of. The first one was when I visited the circus at age three. I was OBSESSED with elephants. We had gone to Sears to buy a special dress for the occasion; it was pink and fluffy and something that I would never put on my own daughter, but at the time I thought it was BEEE-UTIFUL. Unfortunately, halfway through the show, while the elephants were doing their performance thing, I ate my last bit of popcorn, then barfed all over my pink fluffy dress. I remember the shame that flooded over me. And the vivid embarrassment when everyone turned to stare. (I was also upset that the elephants seemed to laugh at me: they lifted their trunks in a very snarky way.)

When I looked back over my memory list as a whole, I discovered that fear of embarrassment was a common thread. And in probably not that great a coincidence, it continues to be a triggering emotion in my life to this day. I'm paranoid about feeling confident because it might invite mockery over something I didn't notice about myself, like a weird hair growing under my chin. I'm certain that anyone who comes to my house has X-ray vision and can see the cat hair clumps under the furniture from four rooms away. And it causes a lot of anxiety when I think about showing anyone my creativity. Paralyzing "don't even bother putting it out there" anxiety.

Whether who I am causes the emotion to be so impactful, or my experiences as a child built up the strength of that emotion in my mind, I can't tell. (Which came first, the scared chicken or the neurotic egg?) But the awareness of the trigger helps me understand my behavior better. Also, it's made me realize I'm not emotionally comfortable with elephants, no matter how friendly they may seem.

When we're able to uncover memories that can help answer the question "*Why do I do that?*" we start to harness the power to change it into "The best way I've learned to deal with this . . ." instead.

In each of the heads, write a strong memory you have from childhood.
Below each one write the ruling emotion of each memory.

Write down how these incidents have affected
who you are today in good AND bad ways.

GOOD   BAD

Do you notice any common threads? Could any of those
threads affect the way you approach creativity?

— — — — — — — — — — — — — — — — — —

Being creative is our natural state. So all the blocks that are keeping us from creating were put there artificially. Even an accidental aside by a parent, like "Art really isn't your strong point, champ" could be a pivotal nudge that steers us off course and silences our creativity. A comment from my brother when I was twelve that "You're so hairy, you have gorilla arms!" resulted in my wearing long-sleeved shirts in the 104-degree Texas summers for years. When another girl at ballet class said to me, "You should hang out with my grandma, she loves embroidering too!" I dropped my hobby of cross-stitching immediately. (Just to be clear, that chick was terrible and had knock-knees, so retrospectively screw her.) No wonder our creative selves tend to be blocked: the world has done its best to block us!

We can easily get sucked into focusing on negatives from the past. (Believe me, griping is one of my favorite pastimes.) But the point of digging up all these memories is not to dwell on them, but to put them to work! "What can I DO with this long-lost fact about myself?" This is most fun to apply in areas where we experienced joy around creativity as a child—because that feeling is what we want to channel NOW. Where did we focus our time when we were free to spend it on our own interests? Drawing? Singing? Dancing? Science-ing? Whether it was a hobby or a subject in school we loved, rediscovering an old passion can be a creative jackpot.

The days I actually cook in my kitchen are few and far between. I consider myself a professional reheater, with a side talent of Postmates. But when I started combing through old photos, I noticed something shocking: cakes. Every birthday, including my own, I would make cakes. Themed cakes. Elaborate cakes. Failed cakes. (Baking powder is NOT baking soda: noted!) I had forgotten that baking was a refuge for me as a kid. The realization was so inspiring, I immediately jumped in the car and drove to my nearest bakery for a dozen cupcakes. All. For. Myself! But, surprise, gluttony is not actually the point of this story.

Recently I had horrendous writer's block. (Actually while I was writing this book, which is the ultimate in irony, getting writer's block while writing a book about releasing creativity.) In a rage, I got out a cookbook and picked out the most elaborate chocolate cake I could find. Five hours later, my mood had flipped from furious to FABU-LOUS! Whipping that sugar and cream, pouring the batter, glazing the cake, squirting out fifty hand-piped flowers (and twenty more into my mouth) got me out of my head and into my heart in a very awesome way. And then, the result made its way into my tummy. BONUS! After channeling that long-lost passion, I was able to jump back into writing with surprising ease. Sugar rush? Who knows, but I definitely keep baking in my creative-outlet arsenal now. Full-body win!

— — — — — — — — — — — — — — — —

List ten activities you used to love doing as a kid.

Now pick one that stands out the most to you.
Do you enjoy this activity in your life now, as a profession or a hobby? What small step could you take to try it out again in your life? Circle the choices below that stand out as the most fun.

GET A BOOK FROM THE LIBRARY!
PURCHASE THE TOOLS!
FIND A STUDY BUDDY!
BRUSH UP WITH YOUTUBE VIDEOS!
LISTEN TO PODCASTS!
TAKE A COMMUNITY COLLEGE CLASS!
HIRE A TUTOR!

SEE A PSYCHIC!
JOIN A FORUM!
FIND A LOCAL CLUB!
CHANGE PROFESSIONS!
GO TO A MUSEUM!
VOLUNTEER AT A NONPROFIT!

Now pick one you circled and try it. Reacquaint yourself with something you used to love. What do you have to lose?

— — — — — — — — — — — — — — —

— — —— — — —— —— — — — —— — — — —

What did you want to be when you grew up? Why?

What was it about the profession that made you dream about it?

Is there an aspect of that dream you can
infuse in what you do for a living now?

We focus on professions as children not because they will give us
status or money but because they seem FUN, pure and simple. No,
we don't have to quit our jobs and become garbage collectors or
Olympic gymnasts to find fulfillment as adults, but it's helpful
to analyze the spark of joy and excitement that CREATED
that dream and deconstruct it for parts to use now!

— — —— — — —— —— — — — —— — — — —

Another area that is beneficial to rediscovering our used-to-be
selves is thinking about objects that were important to us as kids.
Things we collected. Or something we had to cuddle or we melted
down and made our parents' lives hell. (Mine was "lil' blanket." I
still have a scrap stuffed away in a shoebox. When I touch it I calm
down; it's my PMS Kryptonite.)

Collecting things is, on the face of it, a bit odd. I mean, why do it? Are we genetically closer to squirrels than I thought? (Does that explain my crazy overbite?) But when you think about it, collections give us a physical way to reflect our inner lives and interests to the outside world. And they connect us physically to where we've been in the past. "Remember that terrible road trip where we let the lotto ticket fly out of the window and Mom threatened to put us up for adoption? I bought this collectible spoon at the 7-Eleven right before that! Fun times!"

I'm almost embarrassed to admit I collected teapots when I was young.

How that reflects my past inner life, I don't know. Maybe I forgot for a reason. But thinking about that embarrassing teapot collection *could* inspire me to write a Victorian crime novel one day. Or just to drink more tea. Noticing what we paid attention to in the past helps reveal clues about who we are today. We don't need to commit to refreshing long-lost interests, but if something was important to us in the past, it needs to be acknowledged as part of who we are as creators. Yes, deep down I have a teapot fetish, and I'll never be able to shake it, AUGH!

— — — — — — — — — — — — — — — —

Google pictures of toys you loved as a child.
How does seeing them make you feel? Write about how one of them particularly affected you in the past. Print out a picture and paste it in here. If you can actually get your hands on one, all the better!

The more items from our past we can experience with ALL our senses, the better we can feel like a whole creator, in touch with all parts of ourselves.

— — — — — — — — — — — — — — — —

— — — — — — — — — — — — — — — —

What did you collect as a child? Why?

Name some aspects of this collection that resonate with you now.

What creative roads could be opened to you by revisiting this old passion?

— — — — — — — — — — — — — — — —

As we peruse memories of our past lives (as younger selves, not as fighters in a Genghis Khan army or something), things may surprise us in a "Cool!" kind of way. And some, like my bizarre childhood teapot obsession, will surprise us in an "Ugh" kind. Both are useful! It's just as valuable to uncover something we hated as something we loved! OR something we loved but abandoned because we weren't "good at it." That is actually the MOST valuable kind.

We often abandon activities because we're afraid to be bad at them. We're trained as kids to be graded when we learn, so we don't retain the concept of learning for OURSELVES. Instead we carry a fear of being "bad" and judged for it. This promotes risk aversion, which is a huge enemy of creativity. We have to LEARN to be scared of doing something creative. That's messed up! Who knows what we might have stuck with had we just been supported more in our pasts?

— — — — — — — — — — — — — — — — —

List a subject you hated as a child. Why did you hate it so much?
Were you discouraged by peer pressure? Bad teachers?
Or was it simply because you weren't "good" at it?

Now that you are an adult, try something you "hated" before.
Can you find a new freedom in reapproaching it now that you
aren't being judged by others? Or by yourself?

— — — — — — — — — — — — — — — — —

As you paint a fresh picture of yourself as a child,
do you see your past in a different light? What
about young-you surprises you? Excites you?

— — — — — — — — — — — — — — —

That feeling we had when we created as kids with no goal in mind? No pressure? THAT is the feeling we want to capture NOW in our lives as we begin to MAKE things again! Children shouldn't have a monopoly on unconscious joy. We want some too! If we can harness a sliver of that feeling as adults, we will be on the path toward a more creatively fulfilling life.

Always keep in mind: *It is not our fault we stopped creating.* Our inner child wants us to. Desperately! And reacquainting ourselves with our past is a fantastic first step toward doing just that.

The "Now" You

If you were selling yourself on Craigslist, how would you describe yourself? I mean, in the used furniture section, not one of the . . . creepy ones. So think of yourself as a slightly dirty couch and . . . HOLD ON!

Let me start over. Please?

We've done a semi-thorough job perusing our lives from zero until yesterday-ish. If we've dredged up a few memories we can blackmail our relatives with so they'll drive us to the airport without complaint too, bonus!

Now it's time to give ourselves a present with the present! This section focuses on the importance of exploring who we are NOW. What we love. How we see ourselves. How OTHERS see us. We need all these info-bits to build a new Hero-Self who is bursting with creativity, like that weird candy I hated as a kid that gushed when you bit into it. What was it called? Gushers? Nah, that's too on the nose. I'm too lazy to look it up.

Before we dive in, though, let's take a moment to appreciate that *we already have everything we need within us to start creating!* Isn't that nice? No matter what, we're going to ace this test! We own all the tools we need to get us where we want to go. We just have to build up the confidence to access them. And that confidence will come as we figure out who we are NOW, inside and out.

We're basically at that scene in a cop show where the team summarizes what they know about the crime, so the broody star can go, "Aha!" in order for them to go investigate a possible lead. But it's actually a false lead and they end up going to the wrong place or accusing the wrong person, who ends up dead because, uh . . . that's about all I can remember from half-watching *CSI* in the past. At any rate, we're ready to gather evidence about who we are now so we can forge confidently into a more creative future. (This metaphor works, I think!)

Here's a TLDR for the entire section:

Think about an average day. We wake up. Go to work. Come home. Consume stuff and/or pursue hobbies. Go to bed. Fit in a bit of eating and socializing between all other required responsibilities, like making sure our dogs or children get fed as the law requires, rinse, repeat.

But how often do we reflect on HOW we do any of those things? Or WHY?

Most of the time, we take ourselves for granted. We simply . . . exist. Like we ignore the clutter of items in the bottoms of our purses and under our car seats, we rarely examine or question what's going on underneath it all. "How long has that half-eaten muffin been under there? Get me a hazmat suit!"

The good news is that treating ourselves like a research project is one of the greatest joys in life, because truly we are all SO INTERESTING! I mean, if we tried taking ourselves on a date to "get to know" ourselves better, we'd be floored at how many new things we'd discover. (I'm sure we'd hit it off so well, we'd end up attracted to ourselves too. And who knows what that could lead to, wink wink.)

Every time we can identify more about what we ARE or ARE NOT, we come one step closer to harnessing our ability to create. If we don't know what we have in our paint boxes, how can we know all the possible things we could paint? Yes, I am sure a few people just thought in a panic, "What if there's *no paint in my paint box*, Felicia?" I hear you: I'm one of those people too. Catastrophic thinking is my SPECIALTY! It's never a headache, it's meningitis. It's not a firecracker booming outside, it's a nuclear bomb. Rest assured, there's paint. A glorious rainbow of colors totally unique to who each of us are. We just may need a bit more water than others to loosen the crusty bits . . . ugh. *Crusty* is a terrible word. That morphed from inspirational to gross *verrrrry* fast.

Self-awareness is a muscle, and in order to start creating, we must start flexing it. Because the more aware we are of ourselves, the more comfortable we'll be in expressing our points of view. What we like and don't like. What we want to embrace. What we want to shred to pieces with our vengeance!! (Oops.) We need to know and embrace who we are if we want to overcome resistance, criticism, and all the other hurdles that will pop up as we incorporate more creativity into our lives.

— — —— — — —— —— — — —— — — —

SENSES
What are your favorite . . . ?

SIGHTS   SOUNDS

TASTES

SMELLS   TOUCHES

— — —— — — —— — — — — —— — — —

Look at the list of virtues and vices below and write next to each how they apply to you. Circle the ones that MOST apply to you.

VIRTUES	VICES
Faith	Pride
Hope	Greed
Charity	Lust
Fortitude	Envy
Justice	Gluttony
Temperance	Wrath
Prudence	Sloth

(Any Prudences in the house? Holla!)

— — —— — — —— — — — — —— — — —

— — — — — — — — — — — — — — — — —

Write five songs below that are the soundtrack to your life. Play them while you doodle. What does the music bring out of you?

— — — — — — — — — — — — — — — —

Finish the statements below with as many answers as you can think of:

The world needs more:

The world doesn't understand:

If you have a great need to make people understand something, or a deep feeling you want to communicate, that is where you will find the seeds of your most rewarding creativity!

— — — — — — — — — — — — — — —

A fun way we can get out of our own skulls and see ourselves fresh is by treating ourselves as objectively as possible. So get ready to objectify the heck out of yourselves! (In a respectful way, of course.)

There is an allegory referred to as Plato's Cave. It comes from the selfsame ancient Greek philosopher's work, *Republic,* from, oh, nearly 2,500 years ago. If you aren't already familiar with it, I'm excited to drop a maybe-accurate summary of this super-fresh tale into your eyeholes!

Basically Plato (writing AS IF he were Socrates, because ancient Greek philosophy wasn't confusing enough) describes a scenario where a group of people are chained together from birth. Their heads are facing straight forward, they can't move, and they're only allowed to see their shadows against a cave wall their whole life. (These are theoretical people, so don't call the cops yet.) Anyway, the shadows would be the only reality these people know, right? They would, therefore think LIFE is only shadows. <*Insert mind trip.*>

If you were to, say, let one of the women up to walk around outside for a bit, she would be confused and blinded by the outside sun and definitely say, "*WTF why was I chained to that bench all my life?*" But ultimately she'd understand that her previous reality was only a small ASPECT of reality. And if she returned to where she sat (probably kicking and screaming), she'd be able to see her old reality in a completely different way. (Now that I think about it, this is the basic plot of *Unbreakable Kimmy Schmidt*, right? I love that show!)

There are a lot of layers to this allegory that don't really tie in to the point I'm trying to make here because I'm not a philosophy major and this isn't a thesis paper, but what especially resonates with me is the idea of people stepping outside their own reality and seeing themselves with new eyes. Just think about how much we could learn about ourselves from two steps away!

Felicia was a shortish redhead and had a profile that she imagined
looked a little bit like a Gelfling. Her face was kind but nervous,
like a secretary who had a terrible boss who buried her in work. She
was wearing mismatched novelty socks, one with penguins on them
and the other with Sushi Cats, which broadcast to the world that
A) she didn't particularly think growing up was relevant to her
interests, and B) she REALLY liked novelty socks. She tended to
cover her mouth when she smiled, a habit formed before she had her
crooked front teeth fixed, and within the timespan of an hour, she
checked her phone twenty-two times . . .

You get the idea. (Wow, do I really check my phone that often?
Terrible. Work on yourself, Day.)

When writers or actors need to create a character, they build a fictional person bit by bit. "Uptight. Neurotic. Needy. She wants a boyfriend but needs to love herself. She's the kind of person who doesn't like to connect with strangers. Who hates when picture frames are crooked. Who volunteers at the local cat shelter. She probably washes her hands too often and says 'My word!' when things are surprising." (I think I just described my spinster older self, yikes!) Bit by bit they build a fake person until there are enough details that at least on the surface, the character strikes them as believable. One day I was working like this on a character for a TV show, and it occurred to me, *Um, do I know more about this person than I do myself?*

When I analyzed my own real-life character with the same tools I used to build fictional ones, I found some . . . okay, I admit I found some things I didn't appreciate, like "Never replaces the empty toilet paper roll," "Wants external praise a bit too much to be healthy," and "Doesn't bother calling friends to say 'Happy Birthday' if she already gave you a thumbs-up on Facebook." But I also found some things that made me like myself more. "Thinks ideal gift is giving someone else the perfect gift." "Believes in the concept of 'magic' more than a rational person should." "Bit of a glutton. Will drive forty miles for a good macaron." Together, the realizations, even the jokey ones, expanded my sense of self and, in my mind, helped solidify who I am as an artist. With this kind of work, we can all get to know ourselves more objectively. Literally.

— — — — — — — — — — — — — — — —

Film yourself for five minutes. Put the phone somewhere you will (maybe) forget about it. Now watch the video and try to see yourself with objective eyes. Describe the person you see as you would describe a character in a book.

What surprises you about this person?

What does this person's fashion say to others?

What is something you see that you love about this person?

What is something about this person you'd like to change?

If there IS something you want to change, make sure to take the shame out of it. Get excited about making the change. Write down some ways you could do it and give yourself an actionable first step!

— — — — — — — — — — — — — — — —

— — — — — — — — — — — — — — — —

Ask five friends or relatives to give you one sentence that they think describes you as a person. Do their answers surprise you? Please you? (Make you reconsider your relationships?)

— — — — — — — — — — — — — — — —

You are the basis for the starring character of a big summer popcorn movie. Yes, YOU! List five attributes of your hero below, such as "Likes to spend too long in an overly hot shower."

What does the hero WANT?

What does the hero NEED?

What are the hero's FLAWS?

What skills does the hero have that help save the day?

What actor plays YOU?

What does the hero LEARN in the end?

Now name your movie and take a stab at designing
the poster on a separate piece of paper. Use crayons.
Stickers. Do it in Photoshop. Have as much fun as you can
making yourself the star of your own epic movie!

— — — — — — — — — — — — — — —

We can never really know from the outside what's going on inside another person. In some ways that's good, otherwise we'd all be too scared to drive because everyone's faces on the freeway would be twisted in rage like super-scary gargoyles. But we need to be aware of OUR OWN FEELINGS because they're directly tied to how and what we're able to create.

If we feel neutral about our nightmare experiences traveling to Poland with a fourteen-month-old who was teething, why would we care about sharing that experience in a sentence here, like I'm doing now? (It was so traumatic. We had to share a seat. For SEVENTEEN HOURS.) I certainly wouldn't have struggled for so many years making internet videos about tabletop games if I didn't love them so much myself and need to CONVEY that love to other people. "You must love this as much as I do because it's amazing. Let me show you why, I will not stop making these until you AGREE WITH ME!!!" ◄─⊠ See all those exclamation marks? They don't represent apathy, my friend!

The impulse to express ourselves is seated in our emotions. So the freer we are to express them, the more we'll be able to create.

- - - - - - - - - - - - - - - -

FEELINGS

On a basic level, what makes you:

Finish the following sentences:

When I'm happy I   _____.

When I'm sad I   _____.

When I'm angry I   _____.

When I'm afraid I   _____.

When I'm hopeful I   _____.

- - - - - - - - - - - - - - -

In the bookshelf, list your favorite books, games, TV shows, movies, and anything else you LOVE that someone else has created. Survey the collection of your interests. Do you notice any overarching themes you might be drawn to? Feelings? Are these the same emotions you'd ideally convey with your OWN creative work?

— — -— — — — -— — — — — — -— — — —

Take a walk for an hour. Use your phone to snap photos
of anything that makes you FEEL something. And at
the end, delete everything except for one photo.
Why did you keep this photo? How is this the best
representation of you as a creator? What emotion
does it convey that is unique to YOU?

— — -— — — — -— — — — — — —

Even though they're crucial to our creativity, a lot of us fall into patterns of DENYING our emotions. That's because expressing them honestly is discouraged. "Don't cry!" "It's nothing to get angry about." "You're acting really emotional." ("SHUT UP I'M NOT!") When are we actually *encouraged* to express our feelings outside of therapy or watching tear-jerky horse commercials during the Super Bowl? Not often. In fact, our whole lives we're taught to stifle our emotions for the sake of propriety or others' feelings. This makes me sad, because it's certainly not the state we're born into. (Most of us are brought into the world screaming in rage, but let's not work on rechanneling that right now.)

Recently I was at the playground with my baby, and another child came up and wanted to play. After about five minutes, the other mother called the child to leave. Before he left, he wanted to hug my baby good-bye. I asked her, "Do you want a hug?" She looked him straight in the eye, with outrage plastered on her face, and said, "NO!" I'll admit, I winced. I felt the impulse to force her to be polite and accept the hug so the other mother wouldn't think I was raising a heathen. But then I asked myself, *Who am I correcting her for? Myself, other people, or for HER?* So I just smiled and said, "She doesn't want a hug right now, but thanks for offering!" (Needless to say I never saw that other mom again.)

Now, I'm certainly not advocating a *Liar Liar* approach to life. I know my baby eventually will need to learn to be polite and consider other peoples' feelings, but what I don't want is to teach her to cut off what she's feeling for the sake of the outside world before her inner world gets a real chance to develop. It's one thing not to express a feeling, but denying or burying it just causes a toxic sludge puddle we have to excavate later in life through playing too many violent video games.

Being aware of our feelings, letting them flow through and out of us in healthy ways, is an important part of creating a new Hero-Self. And the safest way to release those big emotions we don't know how to deal with is through creating things. We can dance that rage away! Blog that sorrow! Show love to our cat by making tiny animals out of its hair! It's not creepy if we're doing it as an emotional outlet, promise!

Looking at creativity as a release valve for big feelings is a wonderful way to rid ourselves of the inhibition that *I need to be perfect when I make things*. No, we don't. Creating can be *just* a vehicle for releasing feelings. That's just as legitimate as writing an epic novel that wins awards. Sometimes it's even more fulfilling, because it's only for ourselves.

— — — — — — — — — — — — — — —

When was the last time you felt a strong emotion but
denied it for the sake of someone else?

Find a creative outlet to RELEASE and
CHANNEL that emotion! For example . . .
Knit anger into a scarf.
Infuse sorrow into cupcakes.
Share happiness by singing a song.
Dance away your rage about politics.
Do you feel cleansed afterward? Relieved? Lighter?
If creativity is something you use to help clean out your
emotions, with no other goal, that's okay! Don't judge
how you fit it in your life! Just start cleaning!

In a primal way, creating is simply a conduit for showing ourselves to the world. Not necessarily to convince others that we're right, but to be *understood*. This is important to remember when mustering courage to share our weird.

Clearly I'm a huge proponent of being proud of your weirdness. It's in the title of the book. We NEED our weirdnesses. Otherwise the world would be vanilla-flavored boring. (Not to knock vanilla, it's my go-to ice cream flavor. I mean, if you want to fudge-ripple mint-chunk up your dessert, no judgment. For me, give me purity of dessert or give me death.) If everyone had the same opinion about dogs, or summer camp, or glasses . . . if everyone liked the same kinds of food or types of cars, it would be a tragedy, and a betrayal of what nature's given us—an innate uniqueness in how we see the world. (Also it guarantees a near-infinite number of stylish frame choices to help our eyes see. THANKS, MODERN LIVING!)

I'm lucky that I've always been proud to stand out from the crowd. I was homeschooled as a kid, so my weirdness was never bullied out of me like most people's was during their awkward formative years. I was never shamed for embarrassing teen hair choices, something I have ample proof of in old photos. In fact, my inner creator won't even ALLOW me to conform. It insists that I HAVE to stand out—which is a weird sort of reverse peer pressure hipsterdom. (I should probably take my inner creator to group therapy to discuss being a wee bit more flexible, but I'm not sure how to get him/her outside my skull long enough to do an intervention.)

In order to be creative, we need to befriend all parts of ourselves. Our passions and our unique experiences, whatever they may be, need to know they're welcome to join the Us Party, and be reassured that the invitation won't ever be rescinded. "Don't worry. I won't abandon you just because my roommate Dave thinks anime swords aren't good wall decorations." It's worth alienating a few people to free up your creativity. (You were just pretending to get along with Dave anyway.) Hiding who we are takes work. And it's work that betrays who we are. So don't bother!

Our weirdnesses are the most fertile places to start when we want to create. No video ever went viral because people thought, *Gee, I've seen that so many times before, let's share it with everyone I know!* Whatever format of creativity we choose to express ourselves with—whether cooking, welding, creating fake movie props, making our guinea pigs into Instagram stars—by leading with the attributes that set us apart, we will always feel more authentic and more fulfilled in the end.

— — — — — — — — — — — — — — — —

Answer one of the questions below:
On a basic level, why do you think you're weird?
Or—
What are some fun ways you see the world that others don't?
(Hint: IT'S THE SAME QUESTION!)

— — — — — — — — — — — — — — —

— — — — — — — — — — — — — — — — — —

Inside each section of the toolbox below, write a life
experience or interest you have that makes you stand
out as odd compared to the people around you.

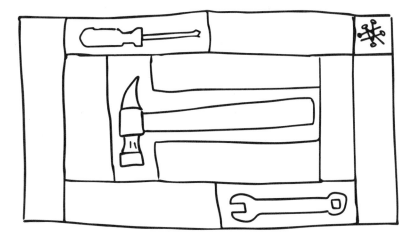

This is your creator toolbox. A place you can always go back to,
where you can find something that will lend your uniqueness to
whatever you want to create! These "oddities" live inside you.
They have ALWAYS lived inside you, just waiting to be shared
with the world. Grab one and see what you can build with it!

— — — — — — — — — — — — — — — — — —

— — — — — — — — — — — — — — — —

Summarize your life in one sentence. What is the title of your autobiography?

What would you LIKE it to be?

— — — — — — — — — — — — — — —

Whatever we take away from this process of rethinking who we are, the wonderful thing to realize is that *there is always so much more we can discover about ourselves!* Anything unearthed here is just the tip of the iceberg! It's so reassuring to be able to own the fact that *I have more creativity inside me than I'll ever be able to express. I'd better start getting it out there now! That mouth harp isn't gonna play itself!*

Dreams

The journey of uncovering our Hero-Selves has taken us through our pasts, our presents, and now into our futures. Where cars fly and all the buildings are glossy and slick! Everyone wears a unitard because we're all SO FIT! We have computers in our skulls! So much neon! There are no trees left! It's like *The Jetsons* gone wild!

Okay, back it up, we'll all be dead before there aren't any trees left. Maybe.

I like to think of myself as a reverse Pig-Pen from *Peanuts*. You know how he carries a cloud of dust around his feet everywhere he goes? That's me, except reverse the placement and substance. Basically I drift through life with my head in the clouds and it's astonishing I get anything done, ever, including this book. (Psst, I'm three months over my deadline!) While I'm thinking of new ways to redecorate my bathroom, I'll drive down a familiar street and, for the first time, notice a twelve-story building. "Wow! That wasn't there yesterday!

They built that quick!" The pile of notes I have on uncracked projects fills four filing cabinets. My New Year's resolutions are generally suggestions, never mandates. And I live in a perpetual state of my brain remarking, "Things are great! But let's imagine how they could be different!" All this used to frustrate me, but then I read a biography of Leonardo da Vinci and took solace in the author's second-guessing: "If only Leonardo had published [whatever], he would have revolutionized the field!" If Leonardo was a dream-filled slacker, there's hope for the rest of us, right?

Except the idea that dreams are a waste of time is infuriating to me. Dreams are the fuel of our creativity! We have to have a restless vision of "else" that makes us get up and MOVE. And those visions are created by our wondering how the world and we, as people, could be different.

So the question is . . .

When you see a random house for sale, do you picture yourself living in it? When you see someone on TV doing something heroic, do you imagine it could be you, if you only had bigger biceps? When you watch a movie, do you dream of being the director, the actor, or the craft-services person who makes everyone's day brighter when they come in with a cart of candy? (Aside: I love Bit-O-Honey and I'm glad everyone else hates it on movie sets because MORE FOR ME!)

No matter how nailed in to our realities we are, we all have things like dream careers, dream vacations, and dream abilities. (Mine is to be able to turn anything into cookies.) To look at the world with possibility-filled eyes is a gift we've been given as human beings, and one that can help us pinpoint at least *a* creative goal to start working toward. That's why making our dreams concrete and actionable is our final step in taking possession of our creative Hero-Self: if you can't dream it first, kids, you'll never achieve it. (THANKS, COACH FELICIA!)

Before goal setting, though, it's helpful to start with the completely impractical. (Not surprising, coming from a consummate daydreamer.) What better way to learn who we want to be as creators than imagining our *ideal* selves? I often picture myself in Meghan Markle's shoes, which is fun for about two seconds, and then I realize she never gets to wear gym clothes to buy coffee anymore and has to be polite to strangers all day *as a job*. Forget that noise.

So try to embrace opening up, taking a chance, and PUSHING the boundaries of what's reasonable or possible for yourself! Hold nothing back!

It might feel like stepping into an icy pool of water to imagine accepting an Oscar on live TV, or seeing a novel you wrote sitting on the shelf of the local library, or landing on Mars to create a colony named after ourselves. (Welcome to Feliciana, "Home of the High-Strung"!) Hubris isn't a quality that's encouraged in life. But we can never know which one of our impractical visions might spawn something life-changing. Might as well imagine in the privacy of our own heads that we CAN do great things! Unless we live in a psychic commune, no one else needs to know about it.

Sure, it probably won't happen for me, but if I allow myself to daydream about winning a gold medal in figure skating, that could spur me to get my own kid skating lessons and give her a chance at winning one herself. (If she wants. Don't worry, I won't be a stage mom, jeez.) If I imagine a world without electrical wires because the area behind my computer is SO TANGLED AND UGLY, no, it probably won't inspire me to go back to engineering school and figure out a way to wirelessly power my Xbox. I honestly don't understand electricity at all. And what's up with the different ends of batteries? Who knows. But I could write the idea into a movie, and perhaps that might inspire a REAL scientist to make it her goal to "make it so," just like Martin Cooper was inspired to invent the cell phone by watching the television show *Star Trek*. (TRUE FACT! LOOK IT UP! CORRECTION! WIKI SAYS THE INSPIRATION WAS DICK TRACY'S WRIST RADIO. MOV-ING ON!)

No matter how ridiculous, go ahead, fling yourself to the stars! There's no gravity inside our imaginations!

As fast as you can, fill the page below with impossible things you could do with your life. Whatever comes to mind. The weirder and more grandiose, the better! Give yourself permission to surprise and delight yourself!

_ _ _ _ _ _ _ _ _ _ _ _ _ _ _ _ _ _

Describe your own superhero outfit.

What superpower would you want?

Why?

How would you improve the world with your powers?

What would be your weakness?

Describe your ideal Fortress of Solitude.

_ _ _ _ _ _ _ _ _ _ _ _ _ _ _ _ _

You suddenly have power over reality. The world of Earth is customized
to your tastes. What is different about it? What would be your ideal
role in it? What favorite fictional things would be a part of it? Things
from past or future ages? How would daily life be different?
(Psst, this could be the start of a great fantasy novel. Just sayin'.)

_ _ _ _ _ _ _ _ _ _ _ _ _ _ _ _ _

For me, I've never NOT had my mood improved by going online and shopping for houses in Barcelona so I can pick one to imaginary-move into. I subscribe to twelve travel email lists so I can more easily picture myself hopping on a plane and going to soak in a hot tub in a fancy South African hotel. (With all the "get out of my house" dreams, I now understand why I like open-world video games so much. It's not about the gameplay or killing things, I'm just looking for exotic places to imagine paying rent.) Will I ever actually live outside my own country? I'd like to think I might retire to a beach in Belize. It's one of my dreams to be an old woman who runs a tourist knick-knack shop and doesn't care about her hair. But if it doesn't happen, maybe just imagining the possibility was enough to inspire me to do SOMETHING creative with my love of travel. (And possibly be able to tax-deduct the whole experience for work, teehee.) At any rate, if we don't allow the "What if?" to exist, then it will never have a chance to affect us or the world. Better to indulge delusions for a hot second than quash something before it can take shape. So open the door and let your dreamer self take over for a bit!

— — — — — — — — — — — — — — — — —

Take a day and go house shopping, just for fun! Go online, browse listings around the world, then describe your dream house below. Bonus for drawing the layout too. (Make sure there are enough bathrooms.)

There are seeds of possibility in each of your dreams. No matter how big or small. And there is nothing NOT worth planting.

— — — — — — — — — — — — — — — —

— — — — — — — — — — — — — — — —

Lightning Round!

I wish I knew how to_____.

I wish I had created/invented _____.

I wish I could spend a year in _____ and do _____.

If I were all-powerful, I would gift _____ to _____.

If I were in _____'s shoes I would _____.

— — — — — — — — — — — — — — —

Your birthday is a global holiday! What does the world do to celebrate?

— — — — — — — — — — — — — —

What have you dreamed of doing that you haven't accomplished
in your life yet? Write those dreams in the clouds.

Visualize them every time you look in the sky.
They are always there above you. Waiting to be actualized.

After allowing our minds to wander and formulate perfectly wonderful impossible dreams for ourselves, a great way to start grounding them in reality is to do what our ancestors did: hold gladiator games!

Just kidding. I meant "hunt and gather." (But if you want to do gladiator games, that's cool. Just don't hurt any animals, please.) When I want to remind myself of what delights me, I pull out a repository of small objects and clippings I've gathered over the years. Pressed flowers. Pictures of hugging platypuses. Weird Al Yankovic's autograph. If it piques my imagination, I collect it. I've done it my whole life. As a kid, I used to cut out my favorite Sunday comics and paste them in a scrapbook. There was a LOT of *Garfield* in there, but strangely, most of the clipped comics involved Nermal. Having a "dream file" full of weird articles about things like the origins of macaron cookies (they were invented by nuns during the French Revolution!) or profiles about people from history I admire, like Nellie Bly, who was a total nineteenth-century badass lady journalist, gives me a place to go for quick creative inspiration and jump-starts my muse.

Whether in a file, in a box, or on Pinterest (YES, IT'S OKAY TO LIKE PINTEREST!), gathering our dreams in one place helps plant them in reality. Sure, the idea of making a "dream board" has become a punch line in sitcoms, but honestly, the first time I made one was the year I started writing *The Guild* and found outside success with my art. So . . . screw it. Go ahead and pin pictures of your dreams on a board! Better yet, try to transform the concept into something more your style. Use a 3-D printer to create a "dream vault." Knit a "dream bag of holding." Solder an adamantium "Aspirational Module of My Alt-Dimensional Existence"! (Okay, that would be too long to print out with a label maker. Also, Felicia, adamantium doesn't really exist. Vibranium? Again, fictional metal. Please stop reading comic books.)

— — — — — — — — — — — — — — — — —

Create a physical space for yourself and your dreams.
Whether using a box, a scrapbook, or services online,
make sure it reflects you as a person. Collect things there
that inspire or excite you as you go through life.
Also write a note to include in your file.
Leave it inside your dream repository for some
future person to find, like in a time capsule.
Describe to them who you are and the purpose of the collection.
And leave them with encouraging words to create
their own collection for their OWN inner creator.
(This is as much for YOU as it is for THEM!)

— — — — — — — — — — — — — — — — —

Once we've cast our net super wide to capture all the dreams we can imagine, the next step is to start turning a few into actionable goals. (If anyone dreamed about growing wings and flying, look up gene-splicing books in the library.) To winnow down the choices, we need to examine each one closely and pose the questions: "Why do I WANT this dream? Do I just want to sign up for the RESULT of it, or do I want to sign up for the PROCESS?" Sorry to have to bring my Mom voice in, but this step is crucial! And requires soul-searching. But answering it in an honest way can guide us closer to defining dreams that will fill our lives with richness rather than frustration. And give us a better chance at achieving them.

When we are able to sign up for the PROCESS of a dream, we have all the power. "I want to put on shows with friends and study to become the best actor I can be! I love the PROCESS of acting!" That dream is actionable! We can incorporate the action of it into our daily lives. Check! But when our dream is "I want to be a famous actor! I want to be glamorous and appear on award shows and travel the world to work on movie sets! And GIVE ME ALL THE FREE STUFF!" Yeah . . . no. That dream puts our hopes in other people's hands. Success there is more based on luck and how straight your nose is than anything else. (Not bitter, promise!)

I'll admit when I first moved to Hollywood, I wanted to be scooped up and lauded for my innate specialness. It wasn't the professional study of acting that motivated me as much as it should have. I was naïve and a wee bit too proud of my cheekbones. And, worse, I placed the power of my dream wholly in the hands of other people, like casting directors and agents and directors. When years went by without my achieving all the external praise I sought from them, I became disillusioned. And I blamed *myself* for not making the dream happen, when, in fact, *I never could have in the first place!* I was approaching it all wrong!

The good thing is, I didn't give up. In fact, failing with the old version of my dream forced me to reevaluate and reaffirm that *Yes, I really do love acting and if I were never successful at it in the way I used to dream about, I would STILL do it because I like pretending and playing dress-up.* So I began to reframe the way I approached my dream to better align with what I, personally, had POWER to make happen. I joined a comedy theater. I started writing my own material to feature myself as an actor. I took class after class after class. By signing up hard-core for the PROCESS of acting, I still, potentially, had a chance to reach the same end result of acclaim and free swag bags, but in the absence of that, I was able to pursue the dream *for* myself *by* myself. It was so empowering! (For the record: still open to free swag bag opportunities.)

If our dreams have built-in engines, then whatever hiccup we encounter we can always keep driving. Whether the dream is "Open a restaurant" or "Speak twelve languages" or "Become the next Steve Jobs," focusing on what we can control is how we will find the creative satisfaction we are looking for. If we're not signing up for the day-to-day work, why bother with that dream at all? We may be neglecting another dream that could lead to more fulfillment and productivity in the long run!

We don't have a right to force other people to hand us our dreams. But we DO have every right to devote ourselves to the *process* of the dream itself. In that way, we are always sure to come out a winner.

And if you realize after digging in that what you've wished for as a creator is more about the praise and fame rather than the actual MAKING of the dream, that's okay! We all do it! (See my writing above.) It's a natural trap to fall into when the world sells us IMAGE everywhere we look. Everyone frames their lives on social media as glorious and uses filters to make their skin perfect. It makes the grind of our own individual *Get those bills paid and underwear washed!* lives seem like a failure in comparison, right? When I'm wiping my baby's poop, I admit I'm a bit envious of people posting pictures of themselves in bikinis at remote beaches. And I think, *What did I do wrong to not be cleaning this poop ON A BEACH right now?* And the answer is, I did nothing wrong. Except focus on everyone's shared ups, and not their hidden downs. (And hidden poop.)

Advertising constantly tells us our metric of "success" should basically involve our being young and wearing a sneer that says, "I have it all and hate it, but at least I'm better than you." We frame our dreams in terms of end results because we only SEE end results. But I promise, even though Kim Kardashian looks like she has it easy-town, it's a chore to do what she does every day. Probably. The writers of *Rick and Morty* don't have everything come easy on the first draft and BAM! create comedy gold (even though it seems like it because it's *so damned funny*). Success follows the grind you love. The daily action you don't regret. The WORST thing you can do is sign up for daily work you hate in order to pursue a dream that's based on what other people control. Because even if you achieve ALL of it, you'll still be pretty miserable.

— — — — — — — — — — — — — — —

List five careers you've dreamt about having.
Think about the day-to-day of each of those dreams. Cross out any that seemed cool at first but the actual work of them seems icky.

Now list five careers you'd NEVER want to have. Why? Sometimes looking at the opposite can help you bring your goals into focus!

— — — — — — — — — — — — — — —

— — — — — — — — — — — — — — —

On this page is a list of sixty creative outlets. Circle the ones that make you excited. Cross out the ones that you'll never do. Put question marks next to ones you hadn't thought of doing but sound interesting to try.

Photography	Knitting	Fencing
Aura Reading	Composing	Woodworking
Cross-	Falconry	Classic Cars
Stitching	Programming	Gardening
Acting	Fashion Design	Magic
Baking	Miniatures	Model Building
Interior	DJing	Quilting
Design	Puzzle Making	Cosplay
Journaling	Rocketry	Game Design
Poetry	Jewelry Making	Decoupage
Scrapbooking	Cooking	Glassblowing
Singing	Poetry	Origami
Vlogging	Watercolor	Woodburning
Filmmaking	Web Design	LARPing
Lassoing	Beer Brewing	Witchcraft
Calligraphy	Genealogy	Stand-Up
Chess	Shoemaking	Podcasting
Digital	Whittling	Soapmaking
Painting	Blacksmithing	Photography
Graphic Design	Accordion	Sculpting
Geocaching	Storytelling	Mad Scientist

Pick one and imagine how you could start incorporating it into your life. Imagine the PROCESS rather than the end result. Does the idea excite you? Congrats on finding a potential creative outlet! If you don't see one that appeals to you, keep searching on your own!

— — — — — — — — — — — — — — — —

What would you do if you won the lottery? Think about your actual NEW daily life. What would you spend your time doing if money were not an issue? How could you start doing one of these things *a little bit* right now?

The need to create is a roiling mass inside us that needs an outlet. But unless we know ourselves, inside and out, we can't truly identify the best way to channel it. Stuck inside, that roiling mass torments us and fills us with tons of heartburn. (I know what I'm talking about, I'm a heartburn expert. I can talk about my acid reflux problems ad infinitum. Just get me going, seriously I'll never stop. What about you? Zantac or Prilosec? Neither? Interesting!) Hopefully, by giving ourselves free rein to dream, and then reining those dreams in to a small number of actionable and exciting goals, we can stop the frustrated roil and . . . begin the boil? Okay, that was terrible. Rephrase:

DREAM IT.
QUESTION IT.
COMMIT TO IT.

Summarize Your Hero-Self

We just took a long journey together in order to build a stronger, more creative Hero-Self. Do you feel more powerful? Whole? I hope so! Rest assured we are glorious phoenixes rising from the ashes of who we used to be. Burning with newfound fiery purpose. We can now begin to blind others with the incandescence of our infinite self-knowledge and imaginations! (TAKE IT DOWN A NOTCH, FELICIA! JEEZ!)

Real talk, my hope is that, after dipping our toes into all the different aspects of who we are, we can now fully embrace the fact that *we are an endless well of interestingness!* And by continuing to explore our pasts, presents, and futures, we can be assured that we'll never run out of things to draw upon creatively!

— — — — — — — — — — — — — — — —

Did anything in this section surprise you about yourself? Add up in an interesting way? Reveal something about your past or present or future that you didn't realize before?

Which ideas made you excited to DO something with them?

— — — — — — — — — — — — — — — —

_ _ _ _ _ _ _ _ _ _ _ _ _ _ _ _ _ _ _

Let's summarize a bit of what we've learned so we can carry
some ideas forward into the rest of our creative journey.

I am _____.

Three adjectives that describe me are

_____, _____, and _____.

I had forgotten I used to be _____.

Something that makes me weird/unique is _____.

Three creative activities that could enrich my life are

_____, _____, and _____.

Three dreams I could enjoy working toward making true are

_____, _____, and _____.

_ _ _ _ _ _ _ _ _ _ _ _ _ _ _ _ _

Great work! Everyone gets a gold star! Like literally, go out and buy some stickers. They're an awesome reward. If anyone is embarrassed at the checkout line? Just pretend they're for your niece or something. No one will check! Anything bought at a crafting store is classified information!

The only thing we have control over in this life is ourselves. Unfortunately, we're not born with user manuals. (Or warranties. Or return slips, for that matter.) So we have to work hard to uncover who we are and what sparks our passions. It's a job. In fact, I believe it's an integral part of the act of living.

And the cool-yet-frustrating part is that we're constantly changing! Every single experience we have morphs who we are into someone new, whether we want it to or not. So our work is never done! It is our constant effort and WILL that defines who we are as a creative person.

— — — — — — — — — — — — — — — — —

Before we finish this section on creating your Hero-Self, let's create something you can take with you, outside of this book. (WARNING: Oovy-groovy gravy ahead!)

On a separate piece of paper, write yourself a fan letter. You are your biggest fan! Let yourself go wild! Gush! Go overboard. Make it so fawning that it makes you smile with the ridiculousness. Then take a big leap and allow yourself to BELIEVE IT. YOU HAVE A RIGHT TO LOVE EVERY BIT OF YOURSELF THIS WAY!

Tuck this letter in a private place where only you can find it. And when you are feeling low, read it out loud. I believe everything you've written. And so could you. No one can stop you from believing in yourself but YOU.

— — — — — — — — — — — — — — — — —

4

ENEMIES

We must shine a light on forces opposing our
creativity so we can banish them with the
strength of our self-awareness. #ByeFelicia

I'm a pretty paranoid individual. Imaginary squirrels are always running under my tires. I always feel like I'm insulting someone with the way I write an email. Heck, I didn't tell my mom I was pregnant until I was eight and a half months along because I didn't want her to freak me out with scary WebMD links. Having her share articles about connections between air pollution and autism or how umbilical cords can do strange things in the womb wasn't going to make this blimp of a preggo sleep any better!

But in the area of being alert for enemies to our creativity, I believe paranoia *does* come in handy.

WAIT!. DON'T GIVE UP!.

I hope I haven't given false hope that channeling our creativity is going to be easy. If I did, I'm sorry; I have an inner cheerleader who's an irritating, chipper little sell-hard. Whatever creative path we embark upon, big or small, we're bound to encounter enemies from within and without. The process is never easy. It's full of stops and starts. Think beatbox versus Kenny G sax. (Tangent, how confident do you have to be to think "professional sax player" could possibly be a viable career path? And as a *sex symbol*? Kenny, thanks for showing us the impossible can become smooth-possible! Haha! I'll stop now.)

However confident and joyful we may be, however modest our

goals, there will always be an enemy ready to rear its ugly head and stop our creativity dead in its tracks. From that inner voice that tells us we're too old to start a career in illustration to that cousin who says we're too chunky to salsa dance. (That cousin is the worst. Seriously, don't bother texting her on her birthday no matter how much your mom tries to guilt you.)

Please know that creating is hard. It is frustrating. And whatever resistance you encounter, *you are not alone.*

I've never created something without the constant torment of an "I feel stuck in emotional molasses and why am I bothering" attitude. If I've ever felt awesome about what I'm working on, it's because A) I've finished completely and am in the process of treating myself to a congratulatory designer purse, or B) I let myself work on something a *wee* bit drunk. (Then the next day I'd read my work over and think, *Wow, this definitely reads like you wrote this drunk.*) Writing, for me, is a constant battle of emotions, ping-ponging between delight as I write one paragraph to total self-hatred as I write another. ◄─ (This one was self-hatred. I ate half a bag of Doritos trying to get through it.)

In this section, we'll identify enemies that stand against us as creators and figure out how to deal with them. One by one. Because we DO have the power to overcome them! We are all Fully Equipped Badass Warrior Creators! (If I could issue official certificates to that effect, I would.) When we are able to understand and identify our own doubts and fears, then our victory will . . . well, it won't be assured. But we can find the strength to keeping TRYING. And that's all we can ask for in life.

I have broken up this chapter into six sections covering nine subjects that can plague our creativity. Partially because they are the most powerful and universal enemies I've grappled with myself, and partially because I'm a mythology nerd and love the visual of a multiheaded Lernaean Hydra standing between us and our goals.

Cool illustration, huh? Thanks, Spencer! If Hercules could chop off all those heads, we can too! (REMINDER: Hercules battled the Hydra because he was paying penance for murdering his wife and children. So . . . don't look too deep into this analogy, please.)

If something resonates in this section, highlight it. If it doesn't, move on. The nine enemies listed in this section may not, in fact, be universal. No list could cover everyone's personal challenges. That's what is so great/frustrating: just as our weirdnesses are one hundred percent unique to each of us, our set of enemies is unique to each of us as well. Yay? But in a way . . . beautiful.

Bottom line, we must work to identify the enemies who oppose our creativity and arm ourselves with the tools to defend ourselves. Because we cannot yield the ground we've gained in knowing ourselves and our creative dreams better! We have too much stuff to say for those jerks to get in our way!

Or, more eloquently . . .

That quote is from the classic work *The Art of War* by Sun Tzu, a Chinese general from 500 BC. Again, awesome illustration, Spencer.

I'll slap that on a tank top, stat. Now let's go start chopping off some heads!

Powerlessness

We can easily fall into the trap of believing that we don't have the power to change our lives. Just like how we can fall into the trap of believing that people on TV are all wearing their own hair. Neither of these things is true. Even I occasionally wear extra hair for acting jobs. I store it in a basket under my sink in an auburn clump. It's scary down there. Like someone melted an orangutan.

In fact, it's frightening how easily a person's sense of free will can be turned into "Meh, why will it matter?" Maybe we were born too shy and anxious to raise our voices. Or found that acting to protect ourselves waved a red flag at people who were abusive or difficult, and it was just easier to constantly give in. (HELLO, *The Devil Wears Prada!*) Maybe it's simply that life gets away from us, and we start to get hemmed in by obligations and careers and family, so we get trapped in a cycle of *I'm not important enough to prioritize!* Especially when we become parents, because babies can't feed or clothe themselves, or seem to put themselves to sleep ever and WHEN ARE YOU GOING TO STOP DRINKING FROM MY BOOBS I REALLY WANT THEM BACK THEY'RE SO SAGGY NOW—

Ahem.

At any rate, powerlessness is one big reason we remain creatively silent. At the core of it, creativity is about expressing ourselves in the unique ways that only we can. But if we don't feel like we have the power to make our voice heard, or if we're constantly waiting for permission to start, well . . . welcome to the Powerless Club! Worst superhero team in history!

I'm someone who's built her reputation on pioneering in web video and creating out-of-the-box content, so it may be strange to hear that exercising agency is difficult for me. I was raised to be so perfect and accommodating that I put everyone else's needs above my own. This mindset affected my creativity in a negative way for a long time. In my early career as an actor, I would constantly look to the director for approval. "Should I emphasize the word 'murder' or 'house'? Just tell me how to say the line, I'm a good parrot!" That's why I got hired for so many commercials. On those sets, actors are treated like meat puppets. "Hold the soup can higher. Smile. Someone get in there with some powder! No, not on the girl, the soup!" When I finally realized, *Oh! Good acting is about the unique choices I make, not what other people tell me is right!* I finally started to think of myself as a CREATOR when I was acting. It was amazing! I could finally emote and stuff! That's why I believe beating back a sense of powerlessness is a key first step in freeing up our creativity.

If we were to list everything about our lives that we'd love to change but haven't, from "the rug in my bathroom" to "working out ever" to "what do I do about rain forest deforestation, I can't stop crying," I'm sure we'd each come up with a very long list. (The rain forest thing is what keeps me awake at night. They're the lungs of the Earth, ya'll! *Why do we keep cutting them down for coffee tables?*) The "fun" fact is that our brains constantly keep track of this "I can't do it" list. That's why, during a sleepless night, I'll suddenly remember that I haven't ever finished that screenplay about my college experiences, which I started FIFTEEN YEARS AGO. Our mind sees all, worries about all. And by carrying around a long list that we feel we can do NOTHING about . . . well, no wonder we feel stagnant and powerless! In the face of ALL OF IT looming over us ALL THE TIME, it's easier to curl up into a ball and binge-watch something terrible but soothing, like five seasons of *Master Chef: Kids*. (Which is actually not terrible, it's FABULOUS and just thinking about it makes me want to give a random child holding a plate of pasta a hug.)

We have to give ourselves the confidence that we can, indeed, change things in our lives. Big and small. And the simplest way to do that is to exercise the power *we already possess* in order to build up trust with ourselves that we can deliver.

My acting teacher, Iris Klein, has a quote that resonates with me every time I think about not replacing an empty toilet paper roll in the bathroom. "The way you do one thing is the way you do everything." (I always end up replacing the toilet paper roll. Even in public stalls. Basically, I'm Mother Teresa.) I love the idea that if we exert power over small things in our lives, we can develop a reflex of exerting power in all the other areas where we may feel stuck.

YES!

WE CAN MAKE AN IMPACT ON OUR WORLD!

YES!

OUR CREATIVITY NEEDS EXPRESSING!

YES!

IT'S WORTH IT TO MAKE THINGS, EVEN IF IT'S A SOCIALLY QUESTIONABLE ACTIVITY LIKE CLOG MAKING!

THE BEST WAY IS TO START SMALL!

LIKE TEENY TINY SMALL. LIKE WITH ITTY BITTY STEPS CAN YOU READ THIS? THAT'S REALLY IMPRESSIVE.

— — — — — — — — — — — — — — — — —

List the ways you feel powerless in your life right now.
Ways as big as your entire career, as small as replacing a broken
light bulb in your closet. List until you can't list anymore. Then go
further! (If you worry about it, chances are you feel powerless about it.)

Now circle ones you can do something about immediately.
Go do one small one *right now!*
How does it *feel?* Amazing, right? Now try another. And
another. This is just the start of feeling powerful enough to
tackle ANYTHING that's holding us frozen! BOOYAH!

— — — — — — — — — — — — — — — — —

A nice way to start practicing being powerful is in the privacy of our own homes. Take a tour to identify physical areas or objects that make you feel powerless. Performing this mental "sniff test" is a wonderful way to help purge things that are psychologically weighing us down. If we're constantly surrounded by disarray and chaos, hemmed in by objects that we endure rather than embrace, it's a signal to our brains that we don't have power to change things. BUT WE DO! We're powerful, creative beings and we deserve organized sock drawers! Yes, I'm saying there's a link between our worn-out socks and our writing the next Great American Novel! Just go with it! Worst-case scenario, we won't grab those annoying socks (the ones with the hole in the big toe) that we keep meaning to replace anymore. Win-win!

Our surroundings are a reflection of our states of mind. So look for opportunities to excite the eye. Because our eyes are connected to our brains. And excited brains feel powerful and spark imaginations! Personally, nothing is more satisfying, and fuels my creativity afterward more, than throwing out all my bras that droop open at the top like a gaping fish's mouth. If something doesn't make my brain buzz, why keep it? *My grandma won't know I threw that vase out, she's dead!* (Sorry, Grandma.) Sure, it sounds dorky, but exercising this kind of power in mundane ways can help us feel, deep in our bones, that we have power over our creativity too.

— — — — — — — — — — — — — — —

Walk through your home and make sure every object passes
the mental "sniff test" of activating your enthusiasm. Does
any object feel like it weighs you down? That you've kept it out
of guilt? You hate it but "one day you might need it"?
Take a box and put all those items in it.
Then put it away in a closet. Out of sight.
If, after a month, you don't miss any of it . . . donate it.
You didn't need it. You deserve to have power over your world!

— — — — — — — — — — — — — — —

Clean out your closet. Purge anything you haven't worn in a year.
Anything that has a bad memory. Anything that
doesn't make you feel powerful and confident.

Even if you're left with a much smaller wardrobe, how do you
feel when you look in your closet NOW versus BEFORE?

Now put on an outfit you usually reserve for looking good for
OTHER PEOPLE and wear it only for yourself. Does it feel self-
indulgent? All right. But don't you deserve your best too?

— — — — — — — — — — — — — — —

Take a room in your house and change five things about it.
You don't need to spend money. Just move a painting in or out of a
room. Move a couch from one wall to the next. Clear a bookshelf
and put a vase and a picture on it instead.

Make those changes, then sit down in the room and look around. Does
it feel different? Does your brain feel more engaged and excited,
seeing something you're so familiar with in a different way?

Take a picture of anything you tweaked to preserve it—as proof
that you ALWAYS have the power to take control over your life.

— — — — — — — — — — — — — — —

Once we are able to assert our power over the immediate world around us, we can move toward exorcising our feeling of powerlessness within the world at large. It's easy to feel guilty when exercising our own agency butts up against someone else's needs. (Yes, I typed "butts." If you giggled, five points.) BUT RESIST THESE EMOTIONS AND DIG IN! If you don't want to go to your friend's cousin's wedding and would like to stay home reading romance novels about broody Highlanders instead, DO IT! We have a right to control our bodies and minds! THEY'RE OURS! WHY DO WE GIVE THEM AWAY SO EASILY? AND WHY AM I YELLING?

When other people ask things of us, something that helps disengage our autopilot of powerlessness is to automatically say:

"I'LL HAVE TO GET BACK TO YOU." ←🖑 Magic words!

Especially on the phone, this has helped me immensely. When I can't see faces, I used to just say "Yes!" to whatever someone was trying to get me to do. I have SO many magazine subscriptions, ya'll. I literally had *Cat Fancy* for three years before I finally unsubscribed because a woman named Pam cold-called me and was really persuasive. So be bold and put the world on pause when confronted with choices about what to do with your own body and mind. We have the right to FREEZE, have a cookie, and ask ourselves, "Which of these choices makes me feel most powerful and protects me more? Okay, let's go with that one. Also, let's have another cookie."

Be judicious. Stand strong. But don't be a selfish jerk. I mean, sometimes you have to bite the bullet and go to your boyfriend's mom's house for dinner. Or not. (You'll definitely have to go occasionally. Sorry.)

_ _ _ _ _ _ _ _ _ _ _ _ _ _ _ _

For the next week, if someone asks you to do something, automatically
make yourself respond, "I'll have to get back to you." Take time to
decide how best to answer for YOURSELF and not for others.
Then list what you did differently than you might have below.

Look at the list. How did exercising your power make you
feel? Like a superstar? Great! Now keep doing it!

_ _ _ _ _ _ _ _ _ _ _ _ _ _ _ _

Don't worry if this proves difficult at first—being powerful takes practice. (Just like being powerless took a lifetime of practice to perfect!) We shouldn't feel bad when we revert to old patterns of behavior. If we can't get a six-pack overnight, why would we be able to get a deep-seated sense of emotional power quickly? Duh! This is a PROCESS! It took years for me to realize that I did NOT have to buy the same dish soap as my mom used to. And that I could BLOCK anyone I didn't like on social media, *even for spurious reasons!* Confederate flag emoji in your Twitter handle? See ya, dickweed! Every tiny step we take to assert our power will be accompanied by inner resistance. But where we persist, we succeed.

It's difficult to create. And that can make us feel . . . *ding ding* HELPLESS! But when we start small and figure out how to approach our creative goals in an empowering way, we can start to do the work. And find the strength to keep it up. Approaching big ideas—like filming a whole movie on our iPhone, or learning to speak Dothraki, or solving the problem of world hunger—can morph from pipe dream to possibility when we demonstrate to ourselves in big ways and small, "Yes! I can be powerful! Let's flex those muscles and start to make this thing happen!"

— — — — — — — — — — — — — — — — — —

Pick one huge item in the world that you feel completely powerless over. Politics. Poverty. Injustice. Brainstorm ten different ways you could take action to tackle your feeling of helplessness around this issue.

Whether you act on this or not, you have demonstrated that you, indeed, have the power to impact something larger than you ever thought you could tackle. ANY amount of action is enough to prove that you CAN make a difference!

— — — — — — — — — — — — — — — — —

‒ ‒ ‒ ‒ ‒ ‒ ‒ ‒ ‒ ‒ ‒ ‒ ‒ ‒ ‒ ‒ ‒ ‒

Download Snap's "I've Got the Power" and just play it on a loop as you
write the title over and over again for the duration of the song.
Just kidding. Except do it anyway. You WILL feel more powerful.
And groovy too.

‒ ‒ ‒ ‒ ‒ ‒ ‒ ‒ ‒ ‒ ‒ ‒ ‒ ‒ ‒ ‒ ‒ ‒

When we demonstrate to ourselves that we have agency over
own lives in small ways, I guarantee that exerting power over bigger
things in our lives seems less intim-
idating. We can feel safe and in
good hands—our own.

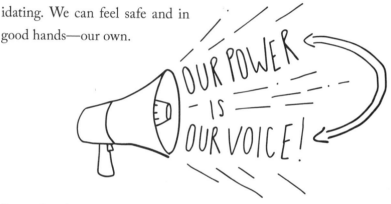

Anxiety

Hey, you know what's awesome?! Feeling like we're drowning in the
panicked emotions of our own out-of-control body after the slightest
stressful encounter with the outside world! It's SO fun to lie in bed
afterward, sleepless and sweating, as we brood over what happened,
positive that a ton of people now despise us! SUCH A FAN OF THIS
STATE OF BEING!

Not.

Real talk. Anxiety is the great enemy of my life. My Sauron.
(Scratch that. Make it my White Witch. At least she had some fashion sense.) It has silenced my voice in so many ways, and sabotaged

my dreams over and over again. At a certain point, I assumed, *Oh, I'm just broken! At least I know myself now!* and I surrendered to the fact that I would never be able to represent my creative work in public as well as I'm able to in the privacy of my own home. (Guys, I sing Boston's "More than a Feeling" so well in the shower, you can't EVEN.) In part, I am writing this book to tell you: I was wrong to give up on myself. There is always hope. There is always a solution. And there is NEVER a good reason to give up on YOU.

Awkward group hug.

Like powerlessness, anxiety is a larger umbrella issue that can encompass way more of our lives than just creativity. But it's able to encompass ALL aspects of our creativity. What a douche of an overachiever, right? It can attack us at the beginning, middle, or end of the creative process. Prevent us from starting. Cause crippling doubt in the middle that makes us want to abandon ship. And strike us with terror after we finish as we think, *What I made is so very very terrible.* It's an underlying cause of a lot of the issues discussed later in the book. Have a creative block? Anxiety is DEFINITELY behind it somewhere, ten layers deep, lurking in a fancy conference room, wearing a very expensive suit, *muhahaha*ing its little heart out. It's like the Illuminati of Enemies! *Why does it torment us this way?*

In order to be creative, we need vivid imaginations—to imagine the impossible, to invent new ways of seeing the world. The flip side of it is that when we're anxious, we're able to use that creativity to imagine all the BAD things that could happen too! Yay! Every bad consequence, terrible rejection, and awful outcome. The more creative we are, the more awful fodder we can come up with to trigger our anxiousness. Awesome/awful, right?

Ironically, the fear that anxiety activates in our brains is also its fuel too. "Oh no. My anxiety is here. I'm afraid. Crap, that just made me more anxious. Which made me more afraid. HELP! I'm caught in a recursive tornado of feelings that I'll never escape and there's nothing I can do about it! TOTO! TOTO!"

The truth is, there are plenty of things we can do about anxiety. We just have to figure out what works for us, individually. And everyone can start with the knowledge that . . .

WE ARE NOT OUR ANXIETY.

It's easy to accept anxiety as a part of who we are instead of separate from ourselves. I did for a long time. "My name is Felicia. I start to hyperventilate every time I'm in large crowds. It's just part of my adorable quirkiness!" Nope. We need to believe firmly and state with a slightly badass edge: "Anxiety is wholly separate from who I am! We are not together. Not dating. Not even hooking up. End of story!"

The "believing anxiety is part of who we are" trap is one reason we've spent so much time building a new, authentic Hero-Self. To establish a baseline of what we TRULY want and what we TRULY feel when we create. When we have a solid, authentic creative identity, we have a much better chance of separating ourselves from our anxiety when it pops up. "Why am I feeling this sense of doom as I try to write a sonnet to my parrot? This definitely doesn't feel like it's coming from my true Hero-Self!" It isn't! Parrot sonnets are universally joyful! By making ourselves understand this fact, deep in our guts, we get on the road to extracting anxiety from our lives. (The fact that anxiety is not who we are, not that parrot sonnets are joyful.)

— — — — — — — — — — — — — — — — —

Think about a recent day when you were anxious.
Approximate the number of minutes you were anxious.

What percentage of that day did you ACTUALLY devote to anxiety?

See? You are NOT your anxiety! It's a teeny-tiny portion of your day.
Just a blip you have to deal with occasionally.
THAT YOU CAN OVERCOME! Rest assured: *it is not YOU.*

— — — — — — — — — — — — — — — — —

Write "I am not my anxiety" over and over below.
As you do, visualize the link between you and this thing
you thought was a part of you peel away.

You are as separate from your anxiety as you are from your shadow.
You may be linked to both, but only YOU are constant.

— — — — — — — — — — — — — — — — —

Before we start into specific techniques to deal with anxiety, let's make ourselves super uncomfortable first. Ready?

Draw your face in the figure below. HUGGING your anxiety.

Now look at it. Really *take in* the idea of embracing
your anxiety. Go as far as saying out loud:
"Thank you for existing, Anxiety. I am so glad I get
to carry you around with me. I love you."

Does the above exercise feel wrong? Strange? Uncomfortable because you're in a coffee shop and it seems like you might be coming across as a crazy person to the people around you? Good! Discomfort is the start of something awesome! (See page 1 in "How to Use This Book." See, I wrote all this stuff for a reason!)

It's probably difficult to embrace the idea of showing love to our anxiety. At first I thought it was repulsive, like eating a stranger's used birthday cake. But treating anxiety with compassion can help us make this a *solvable problem*. It's the universal lesson we learn from movies: if bad guys respond to the mere HINT of empathy, then they're redeemable in the end. (If not, it's fireball-to-the-face time for them!) Our anxiety IS redeemable, I promise. Because IT THINKS IT IS BEING HELPFUL.

Every act of creativity is the brain equivalent of standing at the edge of a hundred-foot cliff and jumping into the unknown. It's ultimately the BEST reward in life, but it also can be scary. And risky. Which invites anxiety to come and "do its thang!" It zings the "fight-or-flight" part of our brains to protect us, because we evolved to see unknown things as dangerous. Better to skedaddle than be eaten by a sabertooth tiger, right? It's weird to think that "learning the trumpet" could equal "sabertooth tiger" in our brains. But it does!

So try to be gentle with your anxiety balloon (and yourself). No one ever went to driving school after someone honked at them. "Gee, they're right, I need to learn how to drive better!" No way. It's middle-finger "Screw you, I'm right!" all the way. Same with our anxiety. If we throw negative emotions at it, our anxiety just tightens up and digs in. What we need is to uncover how to loosen and extract anxiety from our lives, like the terrible parasite . . . I mean, uh, wonderful butterfly it is.

I have studied *so* many techniques for dealing with anxiety. And I would try a hundred more. But the most effective techniques for me when I'm on the spot are the following six. (They go fast, promise!) And when I encounter a stressful situation, I mentally picture pulling out a die and rolling it to determine which of the techniques to use in the moment. Yes, I'm a nerd, if you didn't get that on page one.

Not all of these techniques will work for everyone. But one of them will work for someone, and that alone makes it worth including them all.

FOOL

When anxiety hits us, it's hard to stop. Because it's physiological. The actual insides of our bodies are activated in a different way than our normal states of being. Nerves are zinging, synapses firing. *We can't just stop on a dime!* Not a good idea unless we're playing that motorcycle video game called Trials and want to see our bodies fly off and flop around when we wreck in hilarious ways. (Like, ten of you got that reference.)

But what's only one brainwise step away from anxiety? Excitement! The "hooray we're getting in the car to go to Disneyland!" kind of stuff. Anxiety is almost the same body state as excitement, but our minds are focused on how things could go BADLY rather than WELL. With a bit of mental gymnastics, "I'm so anxious about what's going to happen!" can be flipped into "I can't wait to see what happens!" Just try the opposite to test it out. Try flipping excitement into anxiety!

Except don't, because that would be ruining something nice and let's not do that.

Yes, the aim with this technique is to fool ourselves into thinking a situation we believe is dangerous is, in fact, something safe and guaranteed to go our way. Like when we tell ourselves carob is a perfectly acceptable substitute for chocolate! (It's not.) No, we're not stupid, but we have great imaginations, and visualizing positive outcomes to counter negative outcomes is free of charge and can only help calm us down.

I sometimes use this technique out loud when I have a writing project I don't want to do another draft of because I'm scared I can't make it better. "Hello! I'm so excited to see what problems I get to solve today! I'VE GOT THIS!" (Picture this said in a VERY "bad acting" voice.) It seems a bit silly, but it does work. When used around other people especially, it provides cover for any part of our outer selves that are manifesting anxiety. They'll believe we're excited because we said we were! Fake it till you make it! Or, as Wikipedia says is one of the earliest origins of this phrase:

> So to feel brave, act as if we *were* brave, use all our will to that end, and a courage-fit will very likely replace the fit of fear.
>
> William James (1922)

(That one doesn't roll off the tongue as easily.)

— — — — — — — — — — — — — — — — —

FOOL

Next time you're feeling anxious, compare the feeling to being excited. Close, huh? Now pinpoint the negative outcomes you're worried about. Then consciously flip them to the positive. If you feel sure to fail, assure yourself you're guaranteed success! If you're worried about not being able to solve a problem, say, "Easy. I got this!" Say whatever you come up with out loud: "I am so excited for this! I'm gonna rock!"

Really, what's the worst that could happen by assuming the best for ourselves?

— — — — — — — — — — — — — — — — —

When we're filled with anxiety, we are ANYWHERE but in the moment of where we actually exist—the now. That's weird, right? We shouldn't be PUNISHING ourselves with time travel. But our brains are trying to teach us a lesson to avoid potential future trauma. "Don't enroll in that class! Last time your friend Suzie tried learning a new hobby, she lost a hand to the buzz saw!" So they go hyperactive and start to resemble the stock market floor—where we have no idea what's happening, but it seems like disaster's about to strike because there are *so many people YELLING.*

That's the time for us to back the truck up and *journal it out.*

When we throw a ton of logical answers at our worries, we're able to drain the power from our anxiety. It can't be concerned anymore about, "What will I do?!" We have options! Our inner know-it-all has them all! So go ahead, Hermione that anxiety into the grave.

— — — — — — — — — — — — — — — —

DUMP
Write down every possible solution to a problem you have that is giving you anxiety. Write until your imagination is exhausted. Then write more.
Make sure to put the most ridiculous solutions you can think of on the list. When in doubt, add, "Aliens invade the earth and destroy it." Nothing is so grim you can't unravel it with a little dork-filled humor.

— — — — — — — — — — — — — — —

I have probably two dozen anxiety-dump journals like this in my storage unit. I'm too afraid to throw them in the trash for fear someone will discover them and think I'm a madwoman. (That is not an invitation to break into my storage unit. But if you do, take a box of old taxes and a Rock Band kit. I have way too many of each.)

If we write to the point where we no longer have any solutions that could work, here's the kicker: *Simply accept that there is no solution right now.* And that's okay! We did everything we could! Sometimes accepting that the future is unknown is as big a relief as we can find in the moment. WE CANNOT CONTROL THE FUTURE. UNLESS WE ARE PSYCHIC! AND IF WE ARE, I'VE ALWAYS WANTED TO

BE PSYCHIC, THIS IS SO COOL! We can only do our best, given the circumstances. If we can reassure ourselves of that fact, we can better accept whatever happens.

— — — — — — — — — — — — — — — — —

PROTECT

Anxiety means we care. We are sensitive people who are full of feeling. We may be Highly Sensitive, in fact. (I capitalized it because it's an actual psychological diagnosis, not because I just capitalize things for no reason. Oh, wait, I do.) This is an amazing attribute! The opposite of this is "an uncaring, insensitive person who doesn't feel anything." A person like that would never delight in sketching lemurs or learning how to whittle their own spoons. Be GLAD not to be that douche nozzle.

But the challenge of being a caring, sensitive person is that we can become overaroused in stimulating situations. When our senses are bombarded with too many unfamiliar things at once, we're pressured in multiple ways, and anxiety can creep up on us. And we might not even notice. I just thought it was natural when I'd feel completely out of control and paranoid at everything that came out of my mouth in crowded situations. "I used the word *typical*, did that sound condescending? Please don't escort me to the door!" Whether working alone or about to go on stage to speak to thousands, I honestly never knew for years that my inner creator just needed a time-out sometimes. When we force ourselves to remain in "dangerous" situations, we start to lose trust. And we panic. So that's when we need to roll our die to "Protect" and swoop in to save ourselves!

By self-advocating when we are vulnerable, we are demonstrating to our delicate inner creator that we care. And that we can feel safe to be creative and vulnerable in the future. I'm not saying that with the whiff of a sweaty palm everyone should run to their cars and drive home from a public event immediately, but simply taking five minutes away from the hubbub to do deep breathing in order to collect ourselves again could mean the difference between a fun creative experience and a full-blown panic attack. (A few times I've rested on one of those weird chaise lounges you find in old-timey women's restrooms. I used to think they were sexist but now I think every bathroom needs one. Even the men's.)

Eventually, if we protect ourselves often enough, our inner creator becomes reassured that we'll ALWAYS have their back. And if we need to remove ourselves from a stressful situation entirely . . . well, that's okay too! I literally walked into a party once, said hi to the host just so they knew I came, then immediately walked out.

Probably don't do that.

_ _ _ _ _ _ _ _ _ _ _ _ _ _ _ _ _ _ _

PROTECT

Try to remember the last time you were in a stressful, anxiety-inducing situation. Think back to a point before things fell apart when you could have excused yourself to take a quick few minutes alone to gather your thoughts again. THIS is where your knight in shining self could swoop in next time! Sword brandished! Jumping in to rescue you!

Below, rewrite what could have happened in some incident in the past with THAT scenario in mind. Make yourself retroactively into your own best champion!

Now that you know what you needed, be more alert for opportunities to protect yourself. Even just knowing there is a safety net there could head off anxious feelings before they start.

— — — — — — — — — — — — — — — — —

BABY

Anxiety is often a result of our attention being ALL ON OURSELVES. It imposes a paralyzing self-awareness that leaves other people's actual feelings out of the equation. Yes, I'm saying anxiety is super self-centered. It thinks everyone is against us. In reality, others are not our enemies. (Mostly.) They're probably all excited to see whatever it is we're doing and totally rooting for us, but it certainly doesn't feel like it when their eyeballs are up inside us or we're imagining how they might receive something we're making *even before we start making it.* Putting our focus on potential cheerleaders is a great way to combat internal panic that blocks us when we try to create.

Since I became a parent, I've realized that, when I'm around my baby, I am not anxious about what other people think of me. I act like an absolute idiot. I tell the WORST stories to her at bedtime, and she doesn't care if my second act has holes in it or if a deus ex machina saves the day. She just loves hearing me talk! And that allows me to free up my imagination, be terrible, and still be loved in the end. (Until she's thirteen, and then all bets are off.) Harnessing that feeling of absolute love, for public speaking engagements in particular, has been a big win for me.

Next time there's an anxiety-inducing task at hand, why not visualize doing it in front of someone who's delighted at everything you do? No judgment! It could be a child. It could be a dog. It could be an imaginary friend named Beavis. Or Butt-head. (Dated reference #53.) Whoever it is, that companion is the only person we're creating for or with. And they love everything we do.

I repeat: They will love us NO MATTER WHAT HAPPENS.

BABY

Think of someone (or something) that you want to bring along in spirit
with you when you create. Who will not judge anything you do but will
be delighted with whatever you come up with. (If you can practice
creating in front of this person in real life, so much the better.)
Now, on a separate piece of paper, write a short acceptance
speech for an award show, where you are being lauded for something
creative you made. Dedicate this speech to your "baby."
Whenever you sit down to create, bring this speech and keep
this person in your mind. Visualize them beside you. They
are thrilled to watch you work, and they LOVE whatever you
produce. They accept you, award or no. Unconditionally.

ROBOT

Sometimes it's so easy to get swept away in the
FEELING of anxiety that it's hard to put the brakes on
and even think of a technique to use. (I really need to
make this die. Check my website.) On those occasions,
we can pull out the robot.

Not the dance, although if that works? PLEASE TELL ME IT
WORKS!

In situations where I'm on the spot and I need to recover quickly,
it's helpful to repeat in my head EXACTLY why I am anxious. "I'm
afraid I'm going to do something stupid and people will think I've
been skating on my reputation." Or "I'm worried that four people on
the internet think I look old."

Then I repeat the phrase *over and over again* and completely rob it
of its meaning.

Like seriously, over and over. And over. And over. And over. And
over. And over. And over. And over. And over. And over. And over.
And over. And over. And over. And over. And over. And over. And

over. And over.

Do you want to stop reading yet? See? It works! Yes, the intention is to bore our anxiety to death. Think being seated at a wedding next to someone's in-laws and having to pretend that your friend's dad's fly fishing trips are fascinating. THAT bored. If we really go the distance, until the words have completely become mush in our brains, our anxiety will have peaced out by then. Who wants to listen to us drone on? Even we don't!

This is a technique that improves with time. It may take twenty minutes of mind-numbing repetition the first several times. Then it might only take ten. Then five. Then one. It's up to our individual bodies how long until we adjust. It may seem like hours, but eventually we can distract and calm that anxious friend in our brain. A barking dog eventually stops if we don't stimulate it. So unstimulate that yappy terrier anxiety by turning its panic into mental mush! Send that puppy to the dog house with a good dose of trick and no treat! Give Puppy a bone to gnaw on and send it to the kennel! It's over, Rover! (Should I go on with the dog stuff? No, everyone is bored now. SEE? IT WORKS!)

— — — — — — — — — — — — — — — — — —

ROBOT

When was the last time you felt incredibly anxious? What exactly were you
worried about? Narrow it down to a sentence. Sometimes the default
of "I am afraid they will hate me" is a good fallback. Then write
the sentence over and over. Until you are in a calm state again.

How long did it take?
If you try it again, does it take less time?
What about the next time? And the next?

— — — — — — — — — — — — — — — — —

CHICKEN

Sometimes I have full-on panic attacks. Mostly
when I'm being stared at by strangers. Fun times! And
the attacks manifest in a weird phenomenon where
I'm simply not in my body anymore. I disassociate
myself completely. I go through whatever motions on

autopilot, no control over my actions, while my "self" floats above the scene in terror. Afterward I feel so helpless, so abandoned and unsafe, that I'm devastated. Worse, no gentle or holistic technique helps. Breathing? Psh. Mantras? Who cares? Center . . . CENTER THIS, JERK! <sob> <eat ice cream.>

Recently I tried something new. Something counterintuitive. And it has worked. Not one hundred percent, but enough that it has become my favorite technique during situations where I know I might lose control completely. Because it is ruthless. It is simple. And it is terrifying.

Take a leap and say, "Aha, Anxiety! You're here! Where were you, slacker? Now we can get started!" In fact, don't just get happy when it manifests, INVITE MORE OF IT TO COME!

DARE your body to make you even more anxious!

WILL your heart to race faster!

WELCOME in everything you're terrified of, and tell it to bring its ugly cousin!

What's the worst that could happen? You could pass out? GREAT! BRING IT! (This reaction might just be me. I always thought it was romantic when people fainted in books and got concussions.) If your hands are trembling, tremble them more. Exaggerate the movement as much as you can. "You call that palsy? I'll show you palsy!" In short, play chicken with your anxiety. See who flinches first. In a weird way, by voluntarily choosing "fight," you counteract the "flight" imposed by anxiety.

It goes without saying that you have to be willing to completely crash and burn if you try this. But if the idea resonates with you, and you're willing to try it on something that isn't career- or life-risking, go ahead! Experiment. Put yourself in an anxiety-inducing situation; see if you can get the better of your anxiety by showing it you're in charge!

- - - - - - - - - - - - - -

CHICKEN

Dive in and confront your anxiety head-on. With every symptom, every paranoid thought, affirm it. Amplify it. Embrace it. Dare it to make you melt into a puddle and crater everything you love into the ground. Be the berserker barbarian who has a big sword and nothing to lose. Does being aggressive and calling your anxiety out help you? Does the exaggerated physicality add to your nervousness or detract from it?

- - - - - - - - - - - - - -

By no means is the above a comprehensive guide to mastering anxiety. I have merely listed the handful of techniques that I have successfully used in my own life. (And apparently, invented a cool die.) Everyone's enemies are unique, so figuring out how to approach our individual issues is an ongoing task, but one that can reap infinite rewards. Some people's anxiety is so deep-rooted or hardwired that professional help is needed. Medication is needed. And THOSE THINGS ARE OKAY TOO! In fact, they're awesome. Join me in pursuing ANYTHING that helps! Why NOT look everywhere when we're suffering? What are we, some weird Greek cult worshiping some god named Deprivitus? IF IT HAS A CHANCE TO HELP, DO IT!

- - - - - - - - - - - - - -

Which of the anxiety techniques in this section
are you most excited about using? Why?

- - - - - - - - - - - - - -

Everyone carries around a balloon of anxiety. *Everyone.* I would love to say that one of these techniques could help us POP our balloon entirely, but after a decade of working on myself, I still have to listen to an anti-anxiety tape every single night before I go to bed. But at least now, when I hear the woman say around the 23:12 mark, "You are a calm and relaxed being, who is protected by the energy of the cosmos . . ." I have a Pavlovian response to stop worrying about paying taxes and just get the hell to sleep.

So if Fool, Dump, or Protect don't work, or if Robot, Baby, and Chicken just seems like a bad anime you stumbled into on Netflix, *keep searching!* Make beating anxiety one of your primary life quests. Don't settle. Because we DON'T HAVE TO ENDURE LIVING THIS WAY!

Let's get it out of the way so we can freely be our authentic Hero-Selves when we create. Be brave and work on becoming the master of that frickin' balloon!

Procrastination/Perfectionism/ Fear of Failure

We've tackled a few of the big guns of our potential enemies— powerlessness and anxiety. We've stockpiled tools to help us deal with them. Check. Check. Where to now, Creative Sherpa?

<drum roll>

It's time for the Trio of Creative Trauma! Originality's Terrible Triumvirate! The Troika Who Torture Ingenuity! The—

STOP USING THESAURUS.COM AND KEEP WRITING PLEASE.

<cymbal crash>

Welcome to Procrastination, Perfectionism, and Fear of Failure! Except UNwelcome, because we don't want any of these creativity-sucking monsters in our lives. Good thing we can learn how to handle them when they pop up, and show them the bottoms of our boots!

These three are all connected in super-dysfunctional ways, layered on top of our core creativity, smothering it, like a thick party dip of awfulness. If we can excavate through each of these issues, we'll finally dig down to the creative beans, the real jackpot!

Procrastination

We all have long-term creative goals we'd like to realize, but we allow everything short-term to get in the way. Let's hear it for the guilt-inducing yoke of procrastination! It's the naggy mother-in-law of emotional afflictions. Rest assured, no one is alone in falling victim to it. Many of us decide to binge *Brooklyn Nine-Nine* instead of learning Chinese brush painting. (In fact, most of us.) Hell, I just tabbed over to my browser to retweet a post about some political thing I immediately forgot about instead of finishing this paragraph. GUILTY!

The concept is not new in the slightest. The ancient Greeks even had a term for it: *akrasia*. Meaning "a state of acting against one's better judgment, or lack of will that prevents one from doing the right thing." I guess tons of people back then would rather have gone out to hear a lyre concert or watch naked wrestling than compose philosophy treatises like good citizens. #justlikeus

We're not fooling ourselves in the least with whatever it is we're doing instead of working on our creative goals. "Oh, gee, I could have been working on my poetry instead of playing iPhone games all night? Totally forgot while I spent the night flinging pigs into the air!" But we fling those pigs anyway! Against our best interests. And once we develop this habit of avoidance, well . . . we get REALLY good at it. Practice makes imperfect! Procrastination starts to suck everything into a quicksand-like vortex of inaction—especially around our creativity. After a while, we realize, "Dude, I'm drowning myself. Very. Very. Slowly."

When something lingers in our lives and goes unacted on for too long, what we're avoiding becomes heavier and heavier until it becomes WAY too heavy to tackle at all. It's like procrastination makes us into mental alchemists, morphing hydrogen tasks all the way down to uranium tasks! (Lightest to heaviest elements, FYI. *<pushes glasses up nose>*) I can't tell you how long "call dentist" has been staring at me from a Post-it stuck to my desktop, but at this point it'll require a nuclear bomb to blast me into scheduling a cleaning. If small tasks like that can build up to be so difficult to get started on, the harder, long-term ones seem impossible. So why bother?

Hold up, Mr./Mrs./Ms. Pessimism! We've already learned from the Powerlessness section that we CAN act! We KNOW we have the power inside us RIGHT NOW to overcome anything! Feel that chestburster of forward energy! If we continue channeling the "I have the power to get stuff done, even if it sucks!" attitude by attacking small things we're procrastinating about, then bigger, weightier items, like "Compose a song to my dead gerbil," will seem that much easier to tackle. Because we are demonstrating to ourselves on every level, "I am powerful enough to tackle any problem. Mundane or creative! This one's for you, precious Squeaky! RIP!"

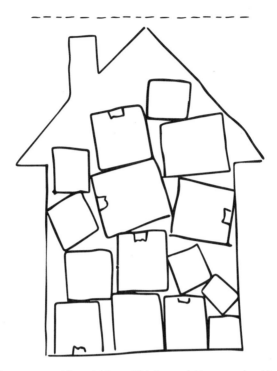

What are you avoiding right now? Write each item on a box blocking you from enjoying your house of creativity. From small to big, from "clean kitchen counter" to "ask boss for raise," put everything on your life to-do list on a box. (Draw new ones if you need to.)

With each item, think about how you can remove this box. Are there some that could be removed more easily than others?

Below, make a to-do list of three of the easy boxes you can start to clear. These are your focus until you complete them. Then move on to three others.

Does making a plan help you feel lighter? Good! You are making space for your creativity. And it will fill up as much space as you offer it. So offer it as much as you can!

Look back at your remaining boxes. What will happen if you simply DON'T DO SOME OF THEM? Draw a box below and write one of the tasks you don't care about in it. Then think: "I give myself permission not to do that task."

Mentally put that box on the curb and walk away.
How does that feel? Are you sad? Put it back! Relieved? Great!
Now, think it through: Can you accept the consequences of
removing a goal from your life entirely? Even one thing on the curb
could free you to concentrate on the boxes you genuinely care
about. And help you start moving them from box to reality.

— — — — — — — — — — — — — — — — —

It's helpful to understand that procrastination is not laziness or shiftlessness. It's often a result of feeling overwhelmed and not knowing where to start. The modern world is not kind to our attention spans. We are not meant to deal with a thousand text messages a day, seven choices of toothpaste, and every kind of TV show known to man. I mean, just the act of browsing Netflix alone gives me a panic attack and I usually end up turning the TV off to knit. With all the things available to eat up our attention, it's much easier to do THOSE than peck away at creating. So we put it off. And off. And off.

How do we overcome THAT?

When we walk across a room, do we fix our eyes on where we want to go and start walking, with no regard to what's between us and that goal? No! That's a great way to trip and break a face. Unless you want to go as a mummy for Halloween and don't want to fake it, don't do that. We complete a journey step by step. The trick to overcoming procrastination is to make every single step toward our goals *actionable* and *within our control.*

Actionable means each step is possible and as unstressful as we can make it. If that means breaking the simplest goal down to hundreds of steps, that's okay. If the goal *Get a drink of water* has the steps *Open cabinet* → *Get glass* and we feel stress between those two? ADD ANOTHER FEW STEPS! *Move hand up* → *Grasp glass* are perfectly fine to shove in there. Because when we reduce the stress of moving from point to point, we make it much easier to attack the next task with confidence.

The other qualifier, *within our control*, means that each step should be something we can accomplish without depending on luck or other people. Goals that are not entirely in our power invite procrastination. "I can't really achieve this step for myself, so come on in, lethargy and bad feelings! Put your feet up on the coffee table and stay a while!"

For example, say our goal is to become an Oscar winner:

Walk down Hollywood Blvd. → *Director discovers me on sidewalk.* → *Win Oscar.*

The last two steps aren't within our power. They involve luck and the actions of others. And the first includes the disgusting stress of visiting Hollywood Blvd. I always feel so sorry for tourists who go there expecting . . . anything but what they get. Sorry, German people. Definitely wear socks with those sandals when you visit.

An amended path that COULD lead to winning an Oscar would be more like:

Study acting. → *Get acting work.* → *Do best work possible.* → *Rinse and repeat while earning great acting roles.* → *Possibly win Oscar but keep doing best work.*

It's fine to have aspirational goals to inspire ourselves with, but if it's not within our power to accomplish on the effort of our work alone, it's not actionable and doesn't make the procrastination-overcoming cut. We can only show up and place ourselves in the best positions to achieve our pie-in-the-sky dreams. THAT'S ALL WE CAN DO. AND IT IS ENOUGH!

Take one of your bigger creative goals and write it on the bottom
of the page, inside the butterfly. In the cocoon, write the most
rudimentary first step you can think of to start accomplishing that
goal—one you could literally do right now. Now start filling in the lines
on the right with *actionable* steps that are *within your control*.
Make the list as long as you need to connect the two. If you
feel discouraged at any point, you broke it down too fast!
If you can do the first step, you have the power to do ALL the steps.
And put yourself in the best place to have a CHANCE at your end
dream. Do you see how easily a path like this can enable you to fly?

The process of breaking down goals can be fun. Honest! *Because it's a creative process in itself!* No one else will break down the steps of a goal from A to B like we do individually, because our vision of what we want to accomplish is unique to us. Yes, we might have to do research, learn skills, even reinvent ourselves to accomplish what we want to accomplish (just that), but by breaking down the steps, we demonstrate to ourselves that each goal is an ACHIEVABLE JOURNEY we could indeed take ourselves on.

In the end, beating procrastination comes down to resource management. Which is, coincidentally, my favorite type of video game. In these kinds of games, the player is given a problem and currency with which to buy tools to deal with said problem. That's it. Simple. Clean. Just like life. Unlike in life, the currency is imaginary gold, the problem is usually orcs, and the tools are fireballs, but aside from all that, the analogy is one-to-one.

Perfectionism

As you read this book, you're reading a version that has been written and rewritten probably a dozen times. Hopefully what you end up with reads effortlessly. (Thanks, editor, copyeditor, illustrator, and a few dozen other people whose job it is to make me look good.) But I can assure you that my first attempt at composing this paragraph was absolute torture. Like running through water. Getting-in-the-car-to-go-to-the-gym-January-2nd awful. I'm doubting myself with every letter I type. I probably just ate a self-pity chocolate and sighed heavily. Why? Because I fall victim to perfectionism. All. The. Time.

Too often, I allow myself to focus on the endgame, dozen-times-rewritten version of a paragraph, and not accept the messy first version as part of the process of getting there. If my prose isn't amazing the first time I put my pen on paper, I feel like a failure. Like, if something doesn't fall out of my head fully formed, like Athena springing out of her dad's skull, I have the attitude, "Hang it the Hades up, lady. You're no god. You're not even a lame-ass naiad."

This is the burden of perfectionism that many of us bear, and it stops creativity dead in its tracks.

— — — — — — — — — — — — — — — — — — —

Draw a circle below.

It's not perfect. You suck. Never draw again.

IS THIS SANE OR HEALTHY?
NO WAY!
BUT THAT'S PERFECTIONISM
IN A NUTSHELL!

— — — — — — — — — — — — — — — — —

— — — — — — — — — — — — — — —

In the space below, write five sentences about a superhero
saving a cat from a burning building. Don't think, just write
SOMETHING FUN AND RIDICULOUS. GO GO GO!

Now rewrite your five sentences. Then do it again.
Rewrite either here or on another sheet of paper over and over
until you are happy with what you wrote. If you aren't excited about
what you're writing, throw it out. Risk throwing out something good
to find something even better.

— — — — — — — — — — — — — — —

— — — — — — — — — — — — — — —

Now let's try something different. Below, write five sentences about a supervillain destroying a city. BUT YOU ONLY GET ONE CHANCE. This work will determine whether you are worthy of being called a creator. Don't mess it up. Honestly, every word needs to be perfect. Don't be stupid and use the wrong words together. Also use an ink pen: don't cheat by using pencil. And use exactly the space allotted too, no more, no less. GO!

How did that exercise feel compared to the last? Terrible? Good! Don't work like that!

— — — — — — — — — — — — — — —

It's tempting to imagine that if we're clothed in the armor of perfection, we'll be able to withstand the slings and arrows of criticism better. "I got it RIGHT! Come at me, brosephs!" The problem is that this armor is SO SO HEAVY. We can't experience the joy of creating while carrying around all that heavy metal. Plate mail went out of fashion for a reason, guys.

Perfectionism is great at throwing up roadblocks in the middle of a creative process (in the form of writer's block), and it's even better at preventing us from starting at all (perfectionism hiding in procrastination sheep's clothing). It is the bouncer guarding the entrance to our Club Creativity. And it will not let us inside the joyful place with great cocktails unless we qualify in one thousand tiny, ever-shifting ways. Basically, it's a dick. And *what does it represent anyway?*

Something that doesn't exist.

Nothing is perfect. Literally nothing. Everything has a flaw. Look at the internet. Someone somewhere can always point out something wrong with ANYTHING. Even Beyoncé. *(Gasp!)*

Nature hates perfection. In fact, we evolved because nature itself is imperfect. Every generation is born slightly different from the last and that process has allowed our species to exist in the version that we do now. But when we use perfection as a benchmark, we're begging to stay stuck in an unnatural holding pattern, without growth or improvement. "I'm perfect as I am now, thanks! I don't want to evolve like Nature wants me to! She's dumb! Look at the platypus, what an idiot!" No wonder the perfectionist mindset feels so wrong. Platypuses are literally the best animals out there!

And what about those rare cases where there are not *enough* flaws in something? The concept "uncanny valley" is a good illustration. This is humanlike objects (usually computer-generated) that elicit certain feelings because they appear so similar to, but not quite the same as, humans. *FEELINGS OF REVULSION! BECAUSE THEY'RE TOO PERFECT!* Is THAT what's holding us back from creating? A need to be repulsive? Back the truck up, because the whole thing sounds NUTS!

The things that make us different are our greatest strengths. That includes our flaws. Our flaws make us unique. Memorable. And they make our creativity worth sharing. Because they make what we create different from what anyone else creates. What a beautiful reason to embrace our flaws rather than rejecting them! Perfectionism is rolling its beady little judgmental eyes right now, but it's true.

— — — — — — — — — — — — — — — —

Make a list of your flaws below. Beside each item write
one thing that is positive about it. If you can think
of more than one positive thing, WRITE IT!

— — — — — — — — — — — — — — — —

What creative work do you consider "perfect" in this world? Write it below.

Take some time to research it. Read the biography of the
creator or the history of how it came to be. How many more
flaws did they have to deal with than you thought before?

Everything is work. Everything is failure. Until it is a success.

— — — — — — — — — — — — — — — —

Nothing comes overnight to anyone. Ever see a contortionist do that thing with their butts on their heads? That didn't come after one hamstring stretch. Your perfectionism has to be taught that creativity is a *process*. It will be dirty. And ugly. And we have to remind ourselves of that fact. Over and over again. How?

What do people who take themselves too seriously hate most? Being teased and subverted. It takes their power of "importance" away from them. I've seen this on Twitter a lot, mostly with people who have anime avatars. So yeah, let's do that!

Perfectionism teaches us the lie that there is only one "right" solution. So open the fire hose and spill out *every single alternate solution there is*. Make it a game. If you're stuck on a painting, take a sketch pad and draw twenty different iterations that move you past the point where you're stuck. If you're writing a novel, write a paragraph ten different ways, then keep writing. See how far you have to go until you start to feel like you're doing good work again. Channel that inner smartass. You know it likes to be channeled!

If experimenting with alternate "real" solutions to a problem doesn't shake perfectionism away and allow you to progress (it can be pretty persistent, like a dog on a beef jerky stick), just . . . be worse. WAY worse! Like, act like you're a five-year-old and the word *fart* is so funny you have to write it over and over again in every sentence. "Fart." Hehe. (Five or not, it's always funny.) During this process of total screw-aroundedness, if you feel Perfectionism leaning over your shoulder while adjusting its monocle a bit (I dunno why I'm visualizing a personality trait as the Monopoly guy, but just go with it), do WORSE WORK! It is perfectly legal to say, "I am going to spend an hour writing the worst poetry in existence." Show Perfectionism that THERE IS NO LAW TELLING US WE CAN'T SUCK. "Pass Go with this, stupid top-hat gentleman!"

— — — — — — — — — — — — — — —

Think of a creative problem you're having. Now write the
WORST SOLUTIONS EVER KNOWN TO MAN BELOW.

Wait, wait . . . It's too good, do worse! I believe
you can be more awful. Get back in there!

How FREE do you feel now? Are you inspired to have fun
coming up with possible REAL solutions to your issues? Could it be
that being "naughty" and reckless and subversive and joyful
makes the hard work of creativity . . . *FUN? GASP!*

— — — — — — — — — — — — — — —

A big challenge with shedding our perfectionism, specifically around creative work, is that we often think of ourselves as "fixed" at birth, coming out of the womb with a set of skills that we're pre-programmed to be good at. If we have to attack our creativity with WORK, well, we must not be talented, so why bother? This is so wrong!

We are not fixed. Everything we do, everything we're exposed to, changes us bit by bit. A fixed mindset about ourselves is incredibly destructive. It also sells ourselves short. To think we can never improve? Why not have more faith than that? We are ever-changeable, magical, awesome creatures. We are fully in control of our destinies and abilities. Yes, go ahead and say it, "I'm a special unicorn who is fully capable of kicking ass!"

Creative work means signing up for the process, not the result. If you take on the creative WORK and sign up for the GRIND, then failure or success will be a moot point: we have already gotten our reward in the DOING of it. So go ahead and DO it!

When I wrote my memoir, I agonized and cried and moaned and ate so many cookies I gained five pounds in a month. Then one day I had an epiphany: *What if I allow myself to feel joy before I start writing this book every day? Would it help? Because right now I hate it.* So every morning after that I sat down and, in a separate file, I TOOK OUT THE TRASH. I wrote stream-of-consciousness, whiny, dumb-jokey observations about life. Half diary entries, half "What should I have for lunch?" musings. I wrote for a minimum of fifteen minutes without stopping. It wasn't about the words at all, it was a process of cleansing. Popping the cork on the wine bottle before pouring out the tastiness. Then, when I started working on my book afterward . . . well, I still ate too many cookies, but I enjoyed myself a thousand percent more than I had before.

When blocked, why not create a daily "Trash" file to dump thoughts into before embarking on a bigger creative project? Write about fear. Write about cats. Anything goes! The words are just fuel to break down the wall between us and our inner Hero-Selves. Delete it afterward. *It never happened.*

Is it a "waste of time" to write stuff we'll throw away in the end? Well, time passes either way, so we can "waste time" being stuck, or "waste time" trying to get past it. I guarantee the time we spend procrastinating on our phones because we're blocked by perfectionism will be much more than the time spent writing in a Trash file. Which act feels more empowering? I mean, taking out the Trash, obviously. Who DIDN'T want to drive a garbage truck as a kid?

— — —— — —— — —— — —— — —— — —

Before embarking on whatever creative venture you want to practice, create a Trash file, whether a physical one in a journal or a virtual one on your computer. Take a set amount of time and write.
Dump out your worries, thoughts, jokes, literally anything you can think of. Then turn back to your original goal.
How do you feel after taking out the trash? Does it make you more eager to start working on bigger things?

— — —— — —— — —— — —— — — —

Below is a stone wall. It's what is keeping you from your creative goals. The only way to get through it is to heave everything you can at it until it crumbles and lets you through. Draw as much as you possibly can over the wall, write on it, weigh it down with every word you can think of. Write so much over the words you've already laid down that the wall turns inky and black from so many layers on layers. Once you have thrown everything you can on the wall, start drawing cracks in it. It is cracking! You are making it crumble! Your strength is incredible! BREAK THAT WALL!

See? YOU HAVE THE POWER TO GET
THROUGH ANY BLOCK BY *DOING!*

— — — — — — — — — — — — — — — — —

Make no mistake, creating is hard. It's work. But the secret weapon here is that we can DO anything. The physicality of moving a pen on paper, programming games, or soldering giant metal robot sculptures is only limited by our own physical abilities. It's the fear of our quality of work that most often stops us in our tracks. Learn to love the extra work that being FREE welcomes into our creative world!

So, bye, perfectionism! Are we cured yet? Do we have all the tools to begin creating? Can I go to the bathroom now?

Er, no. We still have to dig deeper. Because anything we've solved in the previous sections are just Band-Aids on one of the deepest and darkest of the issues that stymie our creativity. It's time to get in the hole again.

Dig.
Dig.

One more layer down.
Dig.
Ugh. We're here. Gross.

Fear of Failure

Perfectionism, procrastination—these problems have their root in our fear of failure. (Each of which can then trigger anxiety. And powerlessness. See how they're all a swirling vortex of connected awfulness? Our enemies are organized! They must have a Slack channel or something!) No one delays working on something creative because they're confident it's going to be great when they finally get around to it. Underneath the "Gee, this pantry organization is an emergency situation; writing that album of kids' songs can come later!" is a pulsating fear of not being good enough. Of being mocked. Of having the end result we present to the world not be equal to what we visualize in our hearts and our dreams.

Fear of failure is the strongest deterrent to becoming a creative person, so it's time we tackled it head-on.

Fill in the details of the monster below. Embellish it with color. Markers. Tape. Smear chocolate on it. Whatever works to make it feel real and monstrous. (If I could make mine smell like brussels sprouts, I would.) This monster is the representation of our own deep-buried fear of failure.

Look at it and say, "I forgive you for making me afraid. But I can't let you control my creativity any longer." We're taking this monster down!

By making our fear of failure solid and real, even in silly colored-in monster form, we're able to start confronting it. Because when we let our fear of failure operate in a generalized, amorphous way, there's no way to combat it. It's rock-solid now, so we can attack! Not with actual weapons, don't be violent. With . . . LOGIC. In a few words: Spock it out!

Assume your fear's worst fear will come true. For example, start with, "My creativity is not good enough." What then? Do we quit? Or continue? Well, quitting would make us sad and empty and unfulfilled. We can't quit! Also, why else did we buy this book? So we will keep creating. Check.

Then what? If we keep creating, we'll get better. What if we don't get better? Well, we can study. But what if that doesn't work? Okay, suppose we'll never get better. Do we stop? Yes or no? I don't know! STOP SPOCKING ME! YOUR LOGIC IS REMOVING MY FEAR AND STUFF!

See how the Flowchart of Fear undermines itself? (Worst ride at Disneyland ever!) Fear's strongest weapon is the unknown. So no matter what, the question, "Then what?" can respond to our Fear's attacks and match them. And we are able to demonstrate that we can survive anything. Yes, the battle may CHANGE us, but no matter what, we survive! (Gloria Gaynor was right. Disco has all the answers.)

List your greatest fear in the top left box. Now write
what would happen if it came true in the box on the right.
Keep following the boxes with the mental question, "What then?"
Do you see how there is always a step afterward? You can cope
with anything! *No matter what happens, there is
always a next step. Just. Keep. Stepping!*

WHAT THEN?

WHAT THEN?

WHAT THEN?

As any good gamer or actual warrior can tell you, the easiest way to defeat an enemy is to know their weaknesses. Ice monster? Use a fire axe. Superman? Use Kryptonite. (Wait, that makes us evil, scratch that.) If we're able to attack a vulnerability, BAM! The magic sword is ours. We rescued the prince!

So how do we identify our fear's vulnerability? We give it a name. When we give something a name, it becomes tangible. And <*insert evil laugh*> vulnerable.

We're afraid of failure, but each of us has a unique way that it's activated around creativity. A while ago, I realized that I could describe my own fear of failure this way: "I am afraid that I will not be loved if I mess up." When I hit upon that phrasing, it was like my whole life had been summarized in one sentence. "AHA! So that's why . . . and then I did . . . and of COURSE that makes me . . . DUDE! Light bulb time!" With that, I was able to realize that when I enter situations that expose my creativity, I place my whole sense of self in other people's hands. And if they don't like it, I believe they won't love me. NO ONE will love me. And I hand this power over to people I'll probably never meet again.

Let me repeat again: I constantly hand my heart over to strangers to batter however they wish, and I wonder why I'm constantly wounded all the time, and this makes me reluctant to create. GOOD WAY TO OPERATE? NOT REALLY!

But when we identify the root of our fear of failure, then we can DO something about it. We can create a counterspell. (That's a spell to counter another spell, just to explain that to any nonnerds reading this book.) Compose a sentence or phrase that gives us the power to cut off our fear before it can begin.

Knowing I'm afraid of not being loved if I do something badly, I now prepare myself as I go into situations with the thought, "It's okay, monster. I do not need these people to love me. And if I fail in front of them, I promise I will still love you. And myself." Since I had my baby, I often include her as well. "I will still love my fear if I fail. I will still love myself. My baby will still love me. I should get a dog soon to make it a quorum. But in the end, no matter what happens here—I will be loved."

Whatever phrase resonates, we need to make sure it activates feelings in our hearts and our guts, not just in our brains. It needs to warm us all over, like a hot toddy of emotional acceptance. Only then can our counterspell give us the strength to be willing to fail. In a funny way, *embracing* our fear of failure is the quickest path to reach our joy. There's probably a philosopher out there who said the same thing somewhere. But I googled it with quotes around it and found nothing, so consider that a Felicia Day special!

— — — — — — — — — — — — — — — — — —

What is the root thought behind your fear of failure? Dig deep.
Write until you find a phrase that makes you go "AHA! That's
why I am afraid!" Look for an inner feeling as you write it
that tells you, "Finally! Someone understands me!"

— — — — — — — — — — — — — — — — —

— —— — — —— — —— — — — —— —

Now come up with a sentence that soothes your fear. A counterspell of sorts. One that, when you think it, tames the monster inside you.

No matter what, *you* can always forgive yourself for failing. And love yourself afterward. No one can ever stop you from doing that.

— —— — — —— — —— — — — —— —

Everything creative starts sloppy and terrible and raw. It's like the messiness of raising a pet or a child. We have to guide it and sculpt it as it grows, teach it not to run out into the street and get hit by a car, annoying stuff like that. We can only do our best along the way with the tools we have, and then at a certain point . . . let it go. If what we make has a flaw, it's a beautiful flaw that makes it unique. And guess what? Next time we get to make something new with yet a different flaw! What a beautiful process to discover all the uniqueness we could put in the world!

In looking back over procrastination, perfectionism, and fear of failure, I hope we can all feel more confident in our ability to beat these inevitabilities back when we create. And get to the bottom of the yummy party dip that much faster. We've dug through a lot of layers that have been keeping us stuck and silent. But in the end, all the work will have been worth it. Yum.

Shame/Regret/Jealousy

We're going to VERY briefly stop to survey this group of issues. We don't want to dwell here long for fear of absorbing the toxic, bitchy goo. It's gross here, guys. Like nails-on-a-chalkboard icky. If it was a color, it would be . . . sludge.

These are the mean girls of creative enemies. They fill us with awful negative energy, and underneath they probably all use our mothers' voices, but that, again, is probably better discussed in therapy.

Unlike some other issues, shame, regret, and jealousy don't completely block us from creating, but they do have the ability to taint everything we make. They're like pollution. Yes, we can live with them, but if our insides are being poisoned with every breath . . . why exactly are we hanging out here again?

Let me hammer this home a bit before we continue:

Shame: "I screwed up so bad!"

Regret: "If only I could go back and fix that screwup!"

Jealousy: "Why are THEY allowed to be screwups and not me?"

None of these will ever be supportive bridesmaids. And yet we hang out with them ALL THE TIME! Let's take a tour of our poisons and see exactly how bad each one is for our creativity, shall we?

Shame

Shame is one I like to keep around as a frenemy. I just can't quit it! If I take a bit of time, I can come up with a dozen incidents in my life that will cause my body to flood itself with stress. Seriously, I'll start pitting. In one incident that haunted me for years, I ditched a group of friends in Rome because I randomly ran into another friend who was more famous and I went to a nightclub with her because YOLO! But I was tired and didn't want to drink, which I guess was uncool, so she ghosted me to go hang out with friends who were actual fun, and then I got lost in Rome trying to get back to the hotel, almost got mugged, no one was happy with me, and I spent the rest of the trip self-hate-eating pizza. (As I tell this story, it doesn't actually sound that bad, but at three in the morning when my anxiety is kickin', HOO-BOY, will I get the sweats!)

Shame dredges up memories where we've misstepped or fallen short and *POKE!* reopens those emotional wounds. Over and over again. The act of keeping an incident fresh, ironically, only creates bigger trauma around it. And THAT trauma-on-trauma layering blocks us from being able to move past it. Just like Shame likes it!

Shame is especially harmful when it comes to creativity. When we're too careful, we can't create with any authenticity. But shame ratchets up our fear of failure into overdrive. If we created something imperfect in the past and failed because of it? Don't worry! Shame will never let us forget it!

I had an encounter that racked me with so much shame it took me years to recover. There was a scene in a TV show where I simply couldn't cry. I mean, at first I could. The cameras were rolling, I was feeling it, when, "RING!" someone's cell phone went off. And that was it. My inner artist skedaddled. For every take after that, I couldn't cry. Or feel ANYTHING. Except panic. We finished the scene, everyone was supportive, but . . . nothing. I faked my way through it—and unknowingly, was traumatized by the whole incident. I continued to feel numb for a day or two afterward, and then . . . big sobbing terribleness. I fell into a deep depression. About my career, my creativity, and myself as a person. For MONTHS.

It didn't make sense that I couldn't move past a small incident like that, but the shame was unremorseful. I had to seek therapy and go back to acting 101 class to learn how to do my craft from scratch. I'd inflated the incident until it was so large in my mind that I couldn't work through it alone. I'd trapped myself in a bouncy castle of shame and I couldn't get out!

Yes, making mistakes is the worst. Especially if they are avoidable. But COPING with mistakes is a skill we have to practice in order to create. We need to learn from them, offer forgiveness to ourselves, and move on. That's how we take shame's power away! And open ourselves to the possibility of creating, even after we screw up.

— — — — — — — — — — — — — — — — —

Name an incident in your past that you feel shame about. Where you messed up and it plagues you. If it's around creativity, so much the better!

How does keeping the trauma of the incident fresh
help you? Are you learning something when you remind
yourself over and over how you messed up?
Write down what you can learn from the incident so
you can avoid doing it again in the future. Then at the
end write: "Thank you for this lesson, Shame.
Now I forgive myself."

You have listened. You have learned. Now you're ready to move on.

— — — — — — — — — — — — — — — — —

— — - — — — — — — — — — — — — — —

Sometimes manifesting the emotional into something physical helps
us move on with our lives. In the space below, describe a lingering piece
of shame you can't let go of, no matter what you do.
Then tear the page out and burn it. Watch it disappear.
You're released of this shame. Forever.
You have the power to do this for yourself!

— — - — — — — — — — - — — — — — — —

Regret

Shame is often accompanied by its creepy little pal Regret. "Hehe. Need more torment? I'm here to show you better pasts, and how you COULD be living now." With this new "friend," we get a time traveler AND a psychic in one package! How not very cool!

"Wrong" choices are Regret's jam:

- If only I had started doing *X* earlier.
- If only I hadn't pursued *Y* and done *X* instead.
- If only I had been in the exact spot at the exact time when something miraculous would have happened to me, my life would be so much better. Maybe. I'll never know, though, because I messed up so bad in the past. Congrats!

Regret thrives on the future unreal conditional tense using modal verbs. And how practical does THAT sound? (I spent fifteen minutes googling grammar sites to come up with that sentence. I'm not sure it's accurate but it sounds smart.)

As creative people, we dwell in our imaginations. More than in reality sometimes. So we're particularly vulnerable to indulging Regret. It digs in and polices our actions like a creepy crossing guard of doom.

There isn't a career choice I've made when I haven't wondered, "If I had just made an alternate decision, I'd be so much more successful/rich/fulfilled/unwrinkled right now." I constantly picture myself having followed different paths where I'm running huge corporations or winning awards or being friends with Reese Witherspoon. (I love her book club!) I castigate myself for not having walked through more doors that were opened to me careerwise in the past, and of course, any creative idea I've ever had that I didn't act on was *clearly* the one that would have solidified my name as a writing genius.

Alternate-dimension Felicias are doing SO GOOD! *But how does that help me now?*

In reality, there is no creative advantage to indulging regret. It just makes us more anxious and more scared to make decisions. Because we DON'T WANT regret in our future lives, we are reluctant to commit to a creative path for fear it's not the "right" one. Welcome to Regret Highway! Once you get on, there are no exits!

The thing is, even if we follow the logic of our regrets, and assume we could change the past and fix what we believe were mistakes . . . we would never be able to ensure we'd be happier in the theoretical THEN, either. An equal number of bad things could happen to us as a result of changing the past. As many bad things as good, if we're to believe Dr. Who!

Regret only offers us the scenario of "better." It's a sleazy salesman trying to get us to buy a crappy product with shady science. And in essence, it's telling us, "Everything you have now, even the things you love, are worth throwing away for something different."

— — — — — — — — — — — — — — — —

What do you regret that you didn't do in the past?
Think of something that you believe could have theoretically
changed the path of your life and made you happier.

List five ways that change could have made you
more unhappy than you are now.

NOW list five things in your life that you cherish.
A friend. A job. A creation. A child.

Absorb this thought: Those exact things you love might not
exist without your exact path to NOW. Is all of the above
WORTH LOSING for a theoretical "maybe"?

— — — — — — — — — — — — — — —

I used to be called "Miss Regrets" around my house. But since I had my baby, I've thrown that name out the window. It was very difficult for me to get pregnant. I had many failed attempts, naturally and with science. But I ended up with the perfect baby (objectively). So for me, falling back into a trap of thinking, *Gee, I wish I could go back and change* X . . . means embracing the possibility I would NOT have my exact baby whom I love more than anything.

BACK OFF, EMOTIONAL DINGO! NO ONE TAKES MY BABY! NOT EVEN ME!

Everything that has happened in our lives is so that we can get to the place we are now. And that is the place that leads us to where we *need* to go next. ⬅🦗 Paint that on a Zen garden rock or something.

I can't regret my past because it gave me what I have in the present. I have learned too much, I have loved too much. I have earned my hurt too much. We all have. Yes, our lives would have been different if we had made different choices. Different is not better. It's just different.

But HEYO! Who's showing up now, preventing us from embracing that fact? (Anyone want to sing some Gin Blossoms right now? Anyone get that reference? Okay, just keep reading.)

Jealousy

I might have a tendency to go easy on Shame—after all, sometimes we mess up and there's a reason for it. Regret? Fine, take a moment but move on. But Jealousy is, start to finish, stem to stern, THE WORST!

For one, Jealousy is a big, insecure fat liar. All its power, especially activated around creativity, stems from a place of powerlessness and fear. Underneath, we allow it to make us feel that someone else's success is coming at the expense of our own. It's a small, angry voice hissing inside our skulls, "There is a scarcity of success to go around, and that person has robbed me of my share! *Hiss hiss.*" THIS IS ANYTHING BUT TRUE!

There is no limit to the number of victories we can achieve in this life. Everyone could theoretically find success all at once, and we would still be okay. There is so much abundance in this world! Just go to Costco and see. There's enough Big Mayo for EVERYONE!

This can be hard to wrap our head around, though, when we see someone else living out one of our dreams. I usually have the power to rise above it, but I used to have a "thing" about Zooey Deschanel. She is so cute. She gets all the quirky parts. She sings in a band. And she always dresses in a way that looks chic and oh so cute. I couldn't watch her on awards shows for the longest time without thinking, *I DESERVE THOSE DESIGNER FLATS TOO!*

But the thing is, Jealousy is also dumb. Why covet what other people have achieved? Hello! Our success is tied to who we are. And each of us is weird. *In a good way.* A person's path to success is UNIQUE and therefore ONLY ACHIEVABLE BY THAT PERSON. UNIQUELY! Remember our paragraph about a cat that was the only paragraph about a cat quite like that to ever have existed? If we were to be dropped in the exact same circumstances of other people's lives, body-swap style, we would immediately start making different choices than they would and end up in different places just because we are all different creatures.

The fact is: we can only succeed in OUR world, not someone else's. The RIGHT success for us comes when we are most planted in our own unique weirdness. Jealousy is essentially saying, "I don't like the way I am. So be different and better, me." Thanks for the actionable direction! You should be a life coach! *<insert eye roll>*

Last, Jealousy is lazy. When we envy others, we envy the reward of their efforts rather than the efforts themselves. Anything that we feel jealous about is a result of blood, sweat, and tears. Effort that we may never have enjoyed ourselves at all. Sure, I'd love to have invented Spanx, or sing like Lady Gaga, or have created *Over the Garden Wall*, the greatest animated miniseries in history (nonnegotiable opinion). But when I break down the steps of how each of those creators achieve all those things, I see why I'm not there: BECAUSE I AM NOT THEM AND I DID NOT WANT TO DO THE WORK THEY DID TO GET TO WHERE THEY ARE.

We cannot separate achievement from process. A bit of research on anyone we are jealous of will reveal that no one has it easy. Everyone struggles and is rejected and sobs in the shower every now and then. The question to ask ourselves is: Are we truly willing to endure as many "downs" as the person we're jealous of did to earn their "ups"?

But of course, Jealousy peaces out if actual EFFORT is required. Because it's more of an armchair quarterback than anything. Like I said: the Worst. So the best thing we can do when the catty terror of Jealousy rears its head is focus on ourselves. And on our own uniquely weird creative work. We have to drive our car looking out the front windshield, not constantly staring at the person in the passenger seat. That's what actors do in bad TV shows and I'm constantly screaming as I watch, "YOU'RE GOING TO CRASH, LOOK AT THE ROAD AND STOP EMOTING!"

— — — — — — — — — — — — — — —

Name someone who makes you jealous. Do you envy their fame? Their money? The way people love them? What exactly do you believe you deserve that they have and you do not?

Now think: Do you actually know what their daily life is like? Do some
research! Read their biography. Scroll through their social media.
Be honest: Do you envy the struggles in their lives,
or is it just the accolades you're focusing on?

_ _ _ _   _ _ _ _   _ _ _ _ _   _

So how did you like our survey of emotional poisons? Would recommend? Needs work? Invariably, shame, regret, and jealousy WILL spring up in our lives. There's no getting around it. But there IS an antidote to apply when we start to feel symptoms.

What's the best way to uninvite these forces (and anything else, for that matter) from our brains and get on with our creativity?

GET OUR MOTHER-EFFIN' HALOS OUT!

SAINT _____ IS IN DA HAUS!

In an age of glamorizing antiheroes and mocking anything earnest, it's difficult not to feel dorky diving into emotions that are considered "saintly." If we met Pollyanna on the street, everyone would want to punch her, I get it. But I don't think two millennia of lessons about "good" human qualities is worth throwing out because they're slightly cringeworthy.

If we're able to picture ourselves as virtuous, amazing creatures rising above whatever base enemies are holding us back, we can overcome the toxic stuff. Feel more confident. And a wee bit self-righteous. And that's okay! If it works, use it! Remember how calm Neo from *The Matrix* was when he was fighting three thousand clones? Let's channel THAT badass and see how "dorky" we feel afterward!

Forgiveness—I messed up. It happened. It's okay to move on. (GUT PUNCH)

Gratitude—Thank you for this mistake. The opportunity to learn from it is an opportunity for my growth. (LEFT HOOK)

Generosity—I'm happy to celebrate other people's victories. There is no scarcity of opportunity. We can all succeed, together. (KICK TO THE SHIN)

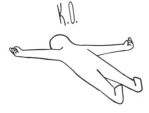

Acceptance—What happened is what needed to happen to get me where I need to go. Any other way is not my path. (KNOCKOUT!)

There's a card game called Magic the Gathering I really love. It has five colors of cards in the deck. The color white is often represented by Angels, who generally wear a smug expression and STOP things from happening in the game. They also protect and enhance those whom they're aligned with. Super irritating, but cool! If a little bit of that smug Angel attitude can rid us of vipers trying to poison our well of creativity, channel it! Picture that halo on our heads, clean white robes swirling around us, and glowy postfacial skin leading the way into our creativity-filled futures.

Shame, regret, and jealousy all have, at their core, a longing to CHANGE. The past. Ourselves. But accepting that we're imperfect, and knowing we have a right to exist anyway, is an empowering and important life tool.

So Shame, Regret, and Jealousy?

SUCK IT!

— — — — — — — — — — — — — — — — — —

In the graphic below, you see a pond full of coins. In each coin, write a wish of success for someone. People you know in real life or people you admire. *ALSO people you hate.* Add more coins and wish for more!

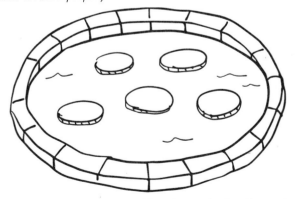

When we activate positive emotions in our brain, they not only counteract the negative, they serve as a reward. So be selfish and think good thoughts! There's literally no downside!

— — — — — — — — — — — — — — — — — —

Real-Life Foes
(Stereotypes/Criticism/Human Enemies)

I recently became addicted to Monty Don, a British TV host who specializes in gardening. Monty is VERY British. Like, he ticks every cliché like *The Big Bang Theory* nails down *nerd*. He likes to gallivant across Europe, showing off the most amazing gardens of the long-dead rich. He strolls through the greenery, spewing elegant commentary, wearing what could only be described as Sherlock Holmes chic. Tweeds. Jaunty caps. A cane that he strides boldly with as if saying, "Grow, beautiful Earth. GROW."

sips tea

eats biscuit

I guess my admiration is for his aura as much as his gardening. He's gentle and positive. It's the opposite of how I approach greenery. For me, tending the outside of my house is a combat sport. I hate getting dirty, but I LOVE killing things. I will deliberately pull a weed as SLOWLY AS I CAN to feel each little root rip away from the life-giving Earth. Half the time I kill as many good plants as bad. I could see myself taking the mower and just CLEARING a whole patch of roses just because there was one dandelion in it. Not surprisingly, no one lets me into the yard unsupervised anymore.

My point is, I've been getting into plants lately (at least watching them on TV) and thought I'd use them to paint a beautiful picture. Imagine looking at our Hero-Selves as a walled garden we've built to grow our blooms of creativity. Up until this point the enemies we've focused on are weeds that could strangle our creations from inside the garden itself (i.e., our brains). But we also have to learn how to deal with external enemies before we harvest our "flowers" and, er, take them to the farmers' market (just hang in with the metaphor, I'm almost finished). Real-life foes could attack our bouquets after we make them and rip them to shreds. Or they might drive their siege engines and fling fire over our walls to burn our crops to the ground before they have a chance to grow at all. I'm not getting hysterical! Don't tell me to calm down! THEY'RE OUT THERE! AND THEY WANT TO RIP APART OUR IMAGINARY CREATIVE FLOWERS! WHAT WOULD MONTY DON DO?

Monty gazes over the destruction. Tuts. "Most unfortunate."

sips tea

eats biscuit

Okay, here's a graphic so we can all absorb how awesome my metaphor is because I WILL NOT LET IT GO.

So how do we protect our garden and our flowers from outside destructive forces? Well, one option is to never show our flowers at all. There's an amazing documentary called *Finding Vivian Maier*

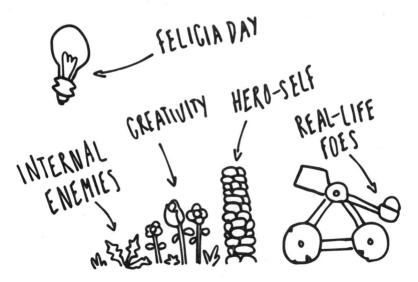

FELICIA DAY

CREATIVITY   HERO-SELF   REAL-LIFE FOES

INTERNAL ENEMIES

about a woman who lived in Chicago from the 1950s to the '70s. She worked as a nanny but, unbeknownst to the world, was one of the most brilliant street photographers out there. Her work was discovered in an unpaid storage unit after her death. Had she shared her work during her life, she might have been lauded. But she died never having done it. Why? Er . . . the film doesn't answer that. Perhaps taking the photos was enough for her? And that's fine! If we want to live a double life like a superhero, accountant by day/secret world-class glassblower at night, no one can stop us.

But creating in isolation isn't enough for most of us. Because, at the heart of it, creativity is about how expressing ourselves affects other people. We want to be understood, we want to share who we are. Whether we try to create great art to last the ages, or just want a cool hobby to talk about at parties, the act of creation is a celebration of our humanity, and it feels wonderful to release it into the world. (If you don't read the YouTube comments. Please never read the YouTube comments.)

In truth, no matter how misanthropic we are, life will have its fingerprints all over our creativity whether we like it or not. We can't create in a vacuum because we don't exist in a vacuum. (We can't, we'd lose consciousness after about fifteen seconds. Oh wait, that wasn't meant to be taken literally.) That's why we have to fight the first of our real-life foes at every turn.

Stereotypes

Our looks and background influence how others treat us more than we can appreciate. In small ways, like our tendency to be-friend people who dress like us, or outright generalizing with stuff like, "Hey, you're tall, you should play basketball!" It's crappy, and messed up. (Especially since I reflexively say that to ALL tall people.) ☹

Society reinforces this concept by propagating "helpful" shorthands to more easily categorize people. This is how we get stereotypes. "My culture tells me that old people are _____. She's _____ because she wears a nerdy T-shirt. He's _____ because he drives that very racy car, and it definitely involves the size of his pee-pee." UGH. PUKE. HURLY HURL.

It takes effort to avoid buying into stereotypes. And even more to defy them. Because people get SUPER ANGRY when called out about their wrong assumptions. It's so weird that people get enraged when offered the opportunity to see other people in a different way, but hey! The world is a bag o' nuts and this proves it!

I generally dress my baby in gender-neutral clothes, because God forbid pink or ruffles ever enter my own wardrobe, and until she asks for alternatives, she's wearing robots, unicorns, and dinosaurs. Nine times out of ten, people assume she's a boy. I never correct them, but I will sometimes say mildly, "Yes, she loves her dinosaur shirts." I've never seen such rage in some random old lady's eyes as when she got my baby's gender wrong. "Why aren't you dressing her in *pink?*" Like I did it to embarrass *her!* Well, ma'am, I don't know you and wasn't aware I needed to cater my baby's existence to validate your assumptions of her at this grocery store today. ALSO THERE ARE THIRTEEN ITEMS IN YOUR BASKET AND THIS IS THE TEN-ITEMS-OR-LESS LINE BUT I HAVEN'T POINTED THAT OUT BECAUSE *I'M* NOT THE RUDE ONE HERE!

When stereotypes are heaped upon us, we may adopt them as part of who we are without noticing. And this can lead us away from our authentic Hero-Selves. Perhaps our gender makes us think we shouldn't take shop or show choir as an elective in school. Or we're dissuaded from a potential creative outlet after hearing things like, "You can't do ballet, your thighs are too large." Or we're pressured into abandoning geeky interests because we're too "hot" (YES, it happens, stop being biased! (😖)). When life tells us to zig, it's hard to zag. But if we always zig, we might be zigging away from who we truly are. Nothing helps our creativity more than a good zagging. (That sounded so dirty. Snicker.)

— — — — — — — — — — — — — — — —

List some stereotypes that accompany you throughout life.
Whether larger things like ethnicity, sex, and race, or smaller
things like being tall, having freckles, or wearing glasses.

What assumptions have been made about you because of them?
How could these stereotypes be affecting your creativity?

— — — — — — — — — — — — — — — —

Stereotypes can also creep in and taint our own creative work because it's much easier to grab low-hanging fruit than the tastier fruit on the higher (more truthful) branches. This is obvious in humor: people are tempted to reach for the very lowest ones for a laugh. "She's undateable because she plays video games!" "He's gay because he's FABULOUS!" NO! Please stop the laugh track and let me off this sitcom!

The good thing is that we already have the tools to deal with this! We're often called "weird" for the very fact that we defy stereotypes in some way. So we can dig into THOSE areas in order to fuel our creativity! For example, the cliché is that often women are not great at math. But I'm a woman who loves math. You can't show me an equation I don't think is hella sexy. Start reading me the quadratic equation and I'll be in my underwear before "2a." Throughout my life I've heard a "That's weird!" response when people learn about it, as if I'd just announced that I'm engaged to a dolphin named Gary or something. (I would never tell people about Gary. I keep my private life private.) I could have let this response dissuade me from loving math and other geeky things. But I didn't. Instead, I was more determined to brandish who I was in people's faces. The only reason I created *The Guild* web series was that I was tired of being judged for playing video games. I wanted to turn people's "That's weird!" reactions into "That's cool!" Talk about MacGyvering a crappy situation!

Only WE can ensure that our creativity resists outside pressures to conform. And in rebelling against stereotypes, we can find enormous power. "You're a girl, you can't write fight scenes with big explosions." YES I CAN! *Here's a rocket to the face to prove it!*

— — — — — — — — — — — — — — —

Name five ways you defy stereotypes.
(Hint: These will often be tied to what you think of as your weirdnesses.)

Brainstorm things you could create that show how you defy them.
For example, an essay about loving something you're "age-inappropriate" for, like quilting or trampoline parks.
The more defiant the creative outlet, the better!

Did any of these ideas make you excited to go try them? To show the world something unexpected? Our best art comes from aiming to change people's minds! (Or channeling spite. That's good motivation too.)

— — — — — — — — — — — — — —

Criticism

After we've made something amazing and authentic that we've put our hearts into, and present it to the world, so delicate and new and precious . . . SPLAT!

We're often hit in the face by CRITICISM.

Remember how squishy and soft the Pillsbury Doughboy is when he presents his baked goods to the audience in the commercials? That's how every creator feels when we offer up our creativity to the world. And when that finger comes in and pokes his soft little belly in the end and he giggles? That's like the criticism we get of our work! Except instead of a fin-ger, it's a knife, and instead of giving a gentle poke, it stabs us in our soft creator bellies and our guts spill out onto the floor. Oh, and we're screaming instead of giggling. Graphic enough? Here's a picture.

Everyone's a critic. In a world of infinite content, people fling arrows of criticism, like Legolas machine-gunning his bow at groups of orcs. (Except not that hot.) Our brains don't know how to appreciate the bounty of creativity we enjoy now. In 1454, there was like ONE lute player. That's all they got. And she was not great and died of the plague. Now we have the equivalent of ten million lute players, five billion troubadours, and a zillion jousters. (Not to mention ten thousand bear baiters on the dark web.) No wonder we dunk on others' creativity without empathy!

When I ran my web video company Geek & Sundry, we needed content. CONSTANTLY. We couldn't generate all the ideas ourselves, so we'd read tons of submissions, each one a precious project that an artist had put their heart and soul into. I could devote maaaaaaybe five minutes to each before mostly saying, "Nope!" and throwing it on the reject pile. At one point I looked over at the discarded stack near my desk and thought with horror, *That foot-high pile is a beautiful vault comprising people's dreams. And I'm about to go shred it.*

We're all guilty of being casual critics. The offhand way I said last week, "I hate Beau Bridges's voice; he sounds like a reanimated teddy bear," made me ashamed after it came out of my mouth. I don't know Beau Bridges. But I do know that making an effort not to throw hate around at his voice might make me go easier on my OWN voice when I accidentally hear myself on a podcast. (Also, a reanimated teddy bear is cool, so why the hell would I hate on that in the first place?) A less critical attitude toward others' creativity is, in the end, better for our OWN creativity.

So when it comes to consuming others' work, our moms were right. "If you can't say something nice, then bring something for everyone and I don't wanna hear it, you're brushing your teeth and then we're going to that twenty-four-hour kung fu marathon at the college so plan on skipping all your classes tomorrow." Oh wait, that's only my mom. Forget it.

— — — — — — — — — — — — — — — — — —

Think of a recent instance when you criticized someone else's work. Were your words fair? Were they NECESSARY?
If you put yourself in the other person's shoes, hearing your own criticism, are you hurt by what you hear?

The kinder we are to others' creativity, the kinder we will be to our own.

— — — — — — — — — — — — — — — — — —

Unfortunately, no matter how hard we empathize with our critics, it's hard to see criticism as anything but negative—because it's a potential danger to our inner creator. "Mom said my pie was gloopy. I'm mortally wounded now. Hold me." *<dramatic chaise longue sobbing>*

When negativity hits us, it can activate our own fears about our abilities. No one gets upset at something they themselves don't fear is true, deep down underneath. That's why I get hurt when someone on Reddit calls me "camel face." I mean, it's not the most INACCU-RATE animal for my facial features. But we have to step away from our personal insecurities and try to see criticism as it is meant to be: a *necessary* result of the act of creation. We made something! And by making something, we sort of asked for it! You can't order a Bloomin' Onion and be surprised at getting heartburn!

The word *criticism* is, by definition "the analysis and judgment of the *merits* and *faults* of a literary or artistic work." Positive AND negative judgment. When we put our work forward, we are *asking* for judgment. We cannot control if that is negative or positive. We can only control the work itself. Is our Hero-Self satisfied with it? Did we put everything we could into it before letting it go? If we didn't, duly noted. Allow one hour to cry. Moving on.

Because at the heart of it, criticism is a gift. Someone used precious moments of their lives to consume a piece of you. Not like a cannibal, that's not a gift, that's murder. Unless they didn't kill you themselves, in which case, it's just highly illegal. I mean they consumed your creativity! You sent something out in the world and they didn't ignore you.

Every piece of our own creativity that we release into the world has the potential to feed the chaos that spurs all *other* originality in the word, butterfly-effect style. (Like chaos theory, not the movie. The movie was . . . it had great cinematography!) So try to reframe criticism through the lens of making a contribution to the collective creativity of the world. Then no matter others' reactions, we have done our part. And we can keep going no matter what feedback we get.

— — — — — — — — — — — — — — — — — —

Below is a set of boxes. In the first one,
insert something you could see yourself creating in the future.
Now fill in the remaining boxes as imaginary stepping
stones between your creation and the bottom box.

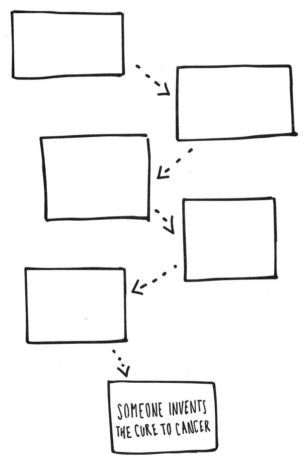

SOMEONE INVENTS
THE CURE TO CANCER

We never know how our creativity will affect others. Everything
has a possible link to everything else. That's why we need to
make as many things as we can. *For the fate of the world!*

— — — — — — — — — — — — — — — —

The truth of it is, resisting criticism is all tied up in our egos, not our actual creativity. When we create expressly for the praise, we feel like we want to commit hari-kari if people don't receive our work like we're the second coming of Michelangelo. Because in doing that, we put all the value in the result, not in the creating itself. But if we do our best as creators every minute of the *process* of creating? A criticism might help us do something better the second time! Like every James Bond villain finds out: the best-laid plans will always be ruined by not properly policing the air vents. The path to improvement is channeling the attitude, "THANK YOU! I can be a BETTER supervillain now! Full crew on air vents, please!" instead of "James Bond ruined my plans by coming through the air vents. Guess I'll hang up the evil laugh and retire to a max-security prison now."

I can't tell you how many times, when I'm writing, I get a FEELING something's not right, but I don't have the tools to dig in and fix it at the time. And rather than dig in harder, I just move on. (Always a bad call. If your inner creator smells rotten fish, figure out where the rotten fish is. It's not going to smell less rotten with time.) Later, if someone points out the flaw I knew was there but I didn't know how to deal with, I feel ashamed. But then I get over it. Because "past me" wasn't equipped to solve the problem. "Two-hours-after-receiving-a-note me" can totally fix it!

— — — — — — — — — — — — — — — —

Think of the worst criticism you've ever received.
The more gutting, the better. Write about it in excruciating detail.
What happened. How it made you feel.

Now think about it from the opposite point of view. How could you
make the criticism WORK for you? Make a game out of brainstorming
ways it could improve your situation or creativity for the better.

Finish by making a list of what you're
PROUD of in your work to counterbalance.

Do whatever it takes with criticism to get
back up and start creating again!

— — — — — — — — — — — — — — —

Everything creative we put out into the world is just a way to figure out how we can be better. Grow more. Be more innovative. Just like test-case Oreos. Candy corn flavor? Gross. Hard pass. But Oreo doesn't close up shop if people hate on one of their experiments, do they? No! They try other things! Like Carrot Cake Oreos! Double blech! NEXT! So look at criticism as other people helping us practice better, that's all. (And it's okay to cry a little too. Just give yourself a two-hour limit, otherwise your eyes will be puffy for a week.)

Human Enemies

Unfortunately, sometimes a person isn't critiquing our work at all; they want to discourage us from creating altogether. There's a wide range of foes like this we could encounter. From those who have their flamethrowers out in an obvious way, to those who sneak matches in their pockets under the guise of "passive-aggressive Aunt Lily and her condescending smile when you tell her you want to go back to school and study interior design." These folks must be anticipated if we want to protect our creative gardens, because they're packing heat and they're heading for our lands!

WHAT DID YOU SAY ABOUT MY HOBBY OF IKEBANA, GRANDMA?! (AKA JAPANESE FLOWER ARRANGING)

I had a great series of sessions with a hypnotherapist once who was an actual accredited professional, not some dude on the corner with a watch on a chain. I went seeking help for audition anxiety. He taught me that, during the act of creativity, we are at our most vulnerable. And we need to try to block the voices of destructive people from hitching a ride with us as we create.

Think about it: football teams never bring cheerleaders along to chant, "Don't screw up! You'll probably screw up! Number thirty-four sucks! GOOO, TEAM!" However innocuous people who harm our creativity may seem, however far away in geography or time, they are always there, lingering. And like garlic breath, their voices inside our heads take FOREVER to go away. The shame they made us feel. (It's described as "burning" for a reason. Hello, flamethrowers.) The mockery. Offhand insults. "Oh, your collages are so *sweet*." They're as powerful as salt on a slug, and they dissolve us over time.

If we try to pretend that something as insignificant as a kid named Trent mocking our drawings in front of the class in fifth grade DOESN'T influence how we approach creativity, then that crap-head will always be lingering in a corner of our brain. Wearing an A&F button-down. Smelling like glue. Sneering at our drawings of dragons in front of the whole class. BEGONE, TRENT! I SEE YOU! AND CAST YOU OUT!

Until we confront them, we can never be free of them.

— —

Think back on your creative past. Were there incidents when someone close to you made you feel ashamed, embarrassed, or discouraged around your creativity? Summarize them in the ghosts here.

Now make up a spell to banish the memories.
As silly or arcane as you want! Read it out loud. Chant.
Burn incense. Make a small ceremony over it. IT IS DONE!
The ghosts can move on now! And so can you!

— —

What helps is to be brave and dredge up the memories and the people involved. Yes, we'd rather bury them six feet under, but go ahead and yank them into a spotlight. And like an FBI agent, interrogate them. "WHERE WERE YOU IN...OH WAIT, I KNOW EXACTLY WHERE YOU WERE. IT'S BURNED INTO ME LIKE A REGRETTABLE TRAMP STAMP. NEW QUESTION: *WHY DID YOU DO THAT TO ME?*" Using a keen, Nancy Drew magnifying glass, we may be able to see the workings of the selfsame demons we battle in our *own* heads in the heads of our real-life creative enemies.

When I first moved to Los Angeles, I took any job I could get. There was a notice in the actor's paper, *Backstage West*, for an independent film. Five roles for girls in their early twenties. (Already a red flag, but hey, I was naïve.) I showed up and was hired by the creator, a brother of a very famous actor. And he NEVER let us forget it. "When my brother was in *X* Oscar-winning film . . ." Blah, blah, blah, BLECH. He would have us improvise, and then TYPE UP the script that WE had made up for him! This guy was terrible. He would have us fetch coffee and get mad if there wasn't enough cream in it. And he was irate when we couldn't make one of the weekly rehearsals that he didn't pay us for. WE DID THIS FOR FOUR MONTHS. After a while I quit. And surprise, he tore into me when I did. "You'll never work in this town again!" was literally said on the phone. And I never saw him again. Well, except ten years later.

I was randomly walking down the street in Hollywood a few years back, and I saw him. And my heart started pounding in fear. Ten years later. I almost ran the other direction. He approached me and I was so frozen I couldn't leave. "Felicia?" He reintroduced himself (like I could have FORGOTTEN) and then . . . apologized. He went on to say that he had not been a good person back then. He had let his demons control him. And substances. And he wanted me to know he was sorry about how he had treated me. Then he left.

I ran back to my car and burst into tears. But they were good ones.

Because, deep down underneath, I realized that working with him had made me wary of collaborating with other people for a long time. And the apology had closed the wound somehow. Would I work with him again? *Hell to the no!* But being able to see him as a flawed human being robbed him of power and reframed the memories. That incident has made it easier for me to look at other negative people as possibly wounded and flawed too. Which in turn, has robbed THEM of power over ME.

There are very few Ramsay Boltons in real life. Just like terrible, "doing it just to harm others" people. Everyone is a hero in their own mind. Whether motivated by jealousy or guilt or regret, people who seek to disrupt our creativity are probably unknowingly motivated by their own enemies working inside them. If we can offer them a little sympathy, then we can rob them of their power over us. They're flawed. Just like we are.

Buuuuut however empathetic we want to be, our creativity is too delicate and vulnerable to allow everyone all-access. That's why a backstage pass at a concert is hard to get: how many randos might show up naked, covered in peanut butter? I'd say a lot if it's a Phish concert. But as long as we're aware, we can draw lines around how we allow other people to interact with our creativity. We can be vigilant in defending and dealing with real-life enemies before they can warp the process of our art.

Sometimes we just need to compartmentalize people a little—even ones very close to us—away from our creativity and give them access only when we are sure not to be vulnerable. If it activates something bad in *them* to be exposed to our creativity, why harm EITHER of us by allowing it to happen?

We are here to sign up for a lifetime of future creativity. Because it will give us joy. And in a variety of ways, for a variety of reasons, others may show up to take that feeling away from us. Life sucks like that.

In the end, we can't control the world. But we can control how we RESPOND to all of it when we're armed with the right tools. When we build strong enough walls to protect our creative gardens. Then our creativity will flourish. And we can offer a glorious bouquet to the world with a smile: "Here is something beautiful that I loved the process of growing. Do with it what thou wilt."

Or in modern terms, "SNIFF THIS, MOFO!"

— — — — — — — — — — — — — — — — — —

List ten people in your life. Beside each name, write how you think each one of them would react to your telling them, "I am a creative person who has unique things to say." Really *imagine* the scene as it plays out, and focus on your imagined emotions as you make your declaration.
With whom do you feel most vulnerable?
Why?

Is there anyone on the list who, no matter how you think about it, will always be a negative force around your creativity? Anyone you would be afraid to show something you put your heart into? Draw them into the doorway below.

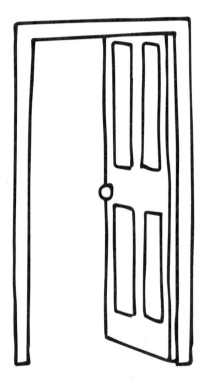

Now close the door.

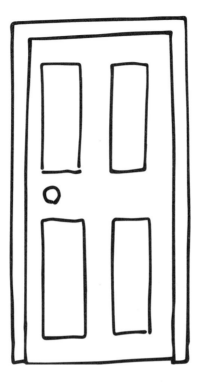

Stare at the closed door. What do you feel?
You have permission to be happy about that closed door!
They can still be in your life, but they aren't THERE
when you create. The door is shut to protect your inner
creator. You have a right to protect yourself!

Summarize Enemies

The training montage is done! We're prepared as much as we can be for enemy assaults on our creativity. We are quote unquote "pumped the heck up." If anything in this section was uncomfortable to deal with, GREAT! That means we hit a nerve. We don't get toothaches for no reason. Something is rotten under there, Hamlet. And whatever it is, we need to muster the tools to deal with it before resorting to emotional root canals. I think that involves rebirth exercises and stuff. It ain't pretty. Let's avoid it if we can, 'kay?

Our creativity is delicate and tasty. Like the smell of fresh-baked bread, it can't help but attract forces that want to devour it. (To be precise, the compound 2-acetyl-1-pyrroline [2AP] makes that fresh, crispy scent. I don't even know chemistry, but boy, is that hawt when it's spelled out.)

There will always be enemies lined up, ready to attack. But now we know how essential creativity is to our lives. As necessary as food and shelter and sleep and game nights. If that means we need to kick mental or physical ass to defend it . . . bring it, world! We are locked and loaded and ready to move on!

Er . . . after we finish the next few pages. THEN we'll be ready.

_ _ _ _ _ _ _ _ _ _ _ _ _ _ _ _ _

Circle the enemy below that seems most likely to
flare up and oppose your creativity:

POWERLESSNESS/ANXIETY/PROCRASTINATION

PERFECTIONISM/FEAR OF FAILURE/SHAME/REGRET

JEALOUSY/STEREOTYPES/CRITICISM/HUMAN ENEMIES

Do you feel better prepared now to keep
creating if and when it arises?
State it to the world!
Complete the statement below:

BACK OFF _____. I AM READY FOR YOU.
            ENEMY
I WILL PUNCH YOU INTO NEXT FRIDAY IF YOU EVEN
THINK ABOUT FLARING UP WHEN I _____!
                                  CREATIVE VERB

With that gauntlet thrown, I'm sure we're all feeling super confident, ready to stride into our creativity-filled futures. BUT WAIT! HOLD UP! SERIOUSLY, STOP. I HAVE ONE LAST POINT TO MAKE!

We've overlooked our most formidable enemy: ourselves.

I recently met a young fan at an event who wanted a picture with me. She wore large, oversized glasses that obscured most of her face. I encouraged her to take them off for a photo. "Oh no. I'm disgusting. I have to leave them on." Wait, *what?* When I pressed her, she got agitated and said even WORSE things about herself. So harsh and wrong. After she left, I was heartbroken. I was at a loss about what I could have said to her to reassure her, "Please don't talk to yourself that way. You are beautiful." But then I remembered—I've talked to myself about my looks, my weight, and my skills in the same hateful way *all my life.*

I envy anyone who walks around loving themselves all the time. Sounds fun. And impossible. We all think horrible thoughts about ourselves on occasion. If not every time we look in the mirror. Or think about our goals while we lie there for hours trying to sleep. *I'm not good enough. No one likes me. I'll never be a writer/artist/musician/ creator. My belly button stinks of Camembert.* We must flush this voice out in the open and deal with it. Now.

Draw yourself as a young child,
two to five years old.
If you can scan a real photo and paste it in,
all the better. Make it as real as can be.
And as cute as you can find.

Now go back and write all the negative things you say
to yourself in bubbles around your child-self. As many as
you can fit around that adorable little picture.

Take that page in. Do you feel bad about it? Of course!
It's child abuse! But this is what we allow to happen every time
we talk to ourselves in an abusive and negative way!

_ _ _ _ _ _ _ _ _ _ _ _ _ _ _ _ _

Every age we've ever lived still exists inside us. And we are most encouraged to feel joy, love, and revel in our creativity when we are children. So when we allow abusive voices in our heads, we are hurting the most vulnerable versions of ourselves. That's why they are able to wound us so badly. Why don't we fight back?!

We all have faults. We are VERY well aware. We don't need to remind ourselves of them constantly. The last thing we need is to allow an enemy to roam free inside us. That's Trojan Horse 101 stuff. Don't fall for it. Instead, take that voice of self-hatred. Those phrases that hurt our most vulnerable selves. And BANISH IT ALL.

Personify every evil thought with a "someone" and crowd them inside the cage below. For every hateful phrase you commonly think about yourself, draw a little monster, or cut out someone's face from a magazine and paste it in, or use stickers, etc.

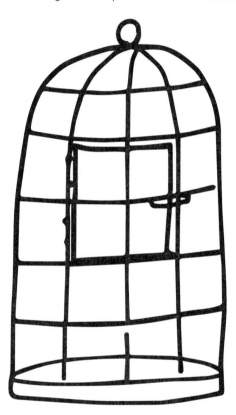

Now visualize hiding that cage in a far corner of your brain where you can't hear those awful phrases. These thoughts are now voiceless. Isolated. Defeated.
They can't hurt you anymore.

NOW we can stride into our creativity-filled futures! Or rather, the next section. Finally!

Seriously. Just go.

ALLIES

In tough times, we need people around us to give us boosts. Like a good bra, they won't leave us hanging.

There's a theory in astronomy called the Drake equation that tries to figure out the exact odds we're not alone in the universe. I'm not going to type it out and scare anyone, but basically it takes the number of stars born per year (Grats! It's a brown dwarf!) and multiplies that by a fraction of increasingly improbable odds of the number of habitable planets, planets that have life, intelligent life, life that can COMMUNICATE, and finally the length of time that it takes for a society to survive and develop the means to communicate with other planets. Whew. The number gets small, guys. Like, decimal and lots of zeroes small. BUT . . . it's always nonzero!

The equation can't guarantee that we'll ever encounter alien life. And the results can vary depending on the numbers you put in, none of which are one hundred percent accurate. Yay, science? But as for ourselves and our own creativity? Felicia's Equation DEFINITELY says we are NOT alone! One hundred percent verified! By me! While I'm typing this!

There are untold numbers of people in the world who are ready to encourage, inspire, and cheer us on. We've sent enough restraining orders out in the enemies section; let's counterbalance that with some nice thank-you cards now!

First an admission: this is a challenging section for me. I have an awkward history with other humans. (This is not a revelation to anyone.) My Twitter bio has read "misanthrope" since 2008. And it all stems from my childhood. My parents homeschooled me and my brother. Which was great, because I slept in every day. The SAT was the first official test I ever took when I decided to apply for college. At fifteen. Until then, I'd only interacted with other children during extracurricular classes. Supervised and structured. No sleepovers. No lunchtime "hangs." No opportunity to be bullied for my weird-nesses, which was good, but also no opportunity to enjoy the concept of basic, human camaraderie. Which was, er . . . bad. I sometimes forget how different my upbringing was from other people's. That is, until a friend invites me out for drinks and I'm like, "What will we be DOING together?" "Uh . . . enjoying each other's company?" "Can I bring a deck of cards so at least we can have the option to play poker?"

I know that growing up separated from other people is the reason I don't reach out for help when I need it. In my mind, I have to do everything myself. That's what being raised in isolation does for you, shocker! It takes effort to remind myself that not all people will make fun of me if I expose my ignorance about boy bands, like some chick named Heather did back in community orchestra. "You don't know who Justin Timberlake is? I mean Joey Fatone is the hot one, but still, what a WEIRDO!" This is probably why, if anyone asks, "Have you seen X?" I always say, "Yes!" even if I haven't. (Confession: I've never seen *Battlestar Galactica*. I HAVE watched compilation trailers just so I could nod smartly if it's brought up in conversation. I've lived a lie.

I'm sorry. End story. Except continue reading.) I have to wage a constant battle with my inner Eeyore, to look outside myself for support, but when I do, it's always worth it. Because I simply wouldn't be here, in any way, shape, or form as a creator, if it weren't for other people encouraging and inspiring me along the way.

It's important to identify other humans who can give us creative boosts. We all need a quick set of favorites in our mental contact list for when our Hero-Self requires guidance and encouragement, or just needs to bitch a little bit about traffic. That's fine too.

I'M SO ALONE...

Role Models

Starting on a broad scale, it's helpful to figure out exactly who our role models in life are and why. Sure, we all have public figures whom we adore. Like, I'm obsessed with Mindy Kaling. (Now that she has a baby, I'm not sure why we're not best friends. I mean we're in the same city and EVERYTHING.) I'm always a bit too focused on what Elon Musk is doing. And Shonda Rhimes. And I see myself in the fictional character of Anne of Green Gables in a completely irrational way. Yes, I'm drawn to these people (or imaginary characters), but WHY? Going beyond hair color or rocket ships, what is something deeper about what they've accomplished that I'm drawn to? (And yes, it's okay to admire someone just for their hair. Not that I would be so superficial. *cough* Amy Adams *cough*)

Figuring out WHY we're inspired by particular people we'll probably never meet can help us learn more about who we are ourselves and what direction we want to go with our creativity. Pinning down that

I'm drawn to Elon Musk for how he revolutionizes things, Shonda Rhimes for how she gives a voice to the underrepresented, and Anne of Green Gables for how she's a quirky, poetry-loving outcast all add up to, "Those are qualities I want to channel on my own journey too! Also, how do I get Amy Adams's hair? The world wants me to have her hair!"

We need people who embody our dreams, shining like pretty little stars in our sky, just to show us that the crazy things we dream about making or doing are actually POSSIBLE. If we've never been exposed to someone like Matt Mercer, who actually makes a living at playing Dungeons & Dragons, then how would we ever get the idea to start playing ourselves? Those imaginary goblins don't get killed by halberds in a vacuum!

It's helpful to do role model role-reversal as well. Have a passion? Pick an achiever! By taking our creative goals and setting out to find people to learn from and emulate, we're able to create a loose outline for how we can accomplish our creative dreams ourselves. We can never duplicate another's path, because of that "each one of us is weirdly unique" thing, but it's nice to have a road map to draw inspiration from and help further define our dreams.

When I was a kid, I had a vague sense that I wanted to be an actor. People thought I was cute and I liked dancing, check! Then I moved to Hollywood to be a REAL actor. Professionally. Er . . . kind of. It took a long time to get my career off the ground. I mostly auditioned for a lot of weepy victim parts. Because that's what was presented to me and I passively accepted it. Had I pinned down exactly whose careers I *actually* coveted and admired before I dove in . . . well, I would have collected the biographies of a lot of dead ladies from old-timey movies (I spent a summer talking in that weird Katharine Hepburn New England accent when I was twelve because that's how I thought movie stars had to talk. It's not.) BUT I also would have picked out a lot of sitcom actors who were funny and not weepy or victim-y at all (except when they wanted to win an Emmy or something). Then I stumbled into a comedy improv class by accident and discovered making people laugh is the BOMB. I was finally able to pin down people like Lisa Kudrow and Megan Mullally as, "HER! I want to do roles like hers! Show me THOSE parts!" Having them as inspiration helped me steer my training and career in a more fulfilling direction. Into hour-long sci-fi television mostly, which is definitey NOT the same as sitcom acting, ahem, but I'm usually the character who cuts the heavy stuff with a quip, so practically the same.

Construct your own personal Mount Rushmore
of people you idolize, living or dead.
Who is on it?
Use photos or paintings to draw them
with as much detail as you can.

— — - — — _ — - — - — _ — - — - —

What person—fictional or real, dead or alive—who inspires
you would you love to have lunch with tomorrow?

Make a list of questions you'd want to ask during the meal
that could help you with your own creative pursuits. Remember
these questions so you'll always have them ready in real-life
situations when you stumble upon someone inspirational!

— — - — — _ — — - — - — _ — - — - —

Write one of your bigger creative goals in the space below.

Now do some research and find a brand-new role model in that field.
How does finding a source of new inspiration excite
you about your own creativity?

— — - — — _ — — - — - — _ — - — - —

However we get there, having a set of people we admire, even if
we never meet them in person, helps draw us forward, like a magnet.

If we ever start to flag on our journeys, we can hold their examples up for a big, juicy boost. "Someone else succeeded! I'm *not* wasting my time! Mmm, tastes like chicken!" And even more than the hope of similar success, being aware of the challenges they faced can help us as creators even more.

We don't see a film crew of six hundred while watching a big action movie; we just watch robots fighting and think that Steven Spielberg's job seems awesome. If we watch *Hamilton*, we consume it in under three hours. In the moment, it's hard to appreciate that it took Lin-Manuel Miranda *six years* to write it. SIX YEARS! If only every piece of art told us the amount of time and effort it took to make, perhaps we'd be a wee bit easier on ourselves when we don't achieve success overnight.

TIME SPENT: 400 DAYS, 16 HOURS, 45 MINUTES, 2 SECONDS
SLEEP LOST: 85 HOURS
TEARS SPILLED: 5 OUNCES

- - - - - - - - - - - - - - - - -

Write a fan letter to a role model who inspires you.
Actually send it.
Your admiration is out there in the world now!
Whether you get a response or not,
you have connected with someone you admire.
Let that be a link that keeps motivating you through tough times!

- - - - - - - - - - - - - - - - -

Mentors

However inspiring Lady Gaga may be as a role model, we'll need a bit of hands-on help to keep us on our creative path. (Unless she's showing up to give you vocal lessons in person. In which case, who are you and can you be MY role model?) That's when we need to turn to *mentors*. Who are kind of like role models, but we can email them the gushiest emails known to man with a lower risk of receiving a restraining order.

When we're kids, we get auto-assigned people to help us learn how the world works. Parents. Teachers. Evil big brothers who throw cheese in our faces. Evolution decided that humans don't get to be like baby snakes, who hatch from their eggs with no guidance at all. Kicked to the curb from birth. Kinda sad. An orphaned baby snake doesn't have any heartstrings-tugging stories to tell. Because it's a snake. ANYWAY, after we're out of school and our parents' houses (or still in them—no shame in saving on rent!), we're kind of expected to . . . guide ourselves? Which sucks, because that's when our hormones are finally in order and we're ready to take advice! Is twenty-fifth grade a thing? I want to enroll, please!

We can't change the fundamentals of human development, but we can seek out people to help guide us through its dark forest. Our inner creator is a constantly growing beast, starving for wisdom. Don't let it go hungry or it'll eat us up from the inside! Er, that's an unnerving visual. Correction: Imagine our inner creator as a cute chibi, who gives us hugs when we feed it ideas. Better? *Whew.*

Most of the time when I feel stuck creatively, I enroll in a class. Any class. Because I know, whoever the teacher is, I will one hundred percent take SOMETHING away from it. I've taken Improv Comedy 101 classes about fifteen times. And always learned new things.

(The last time, with a bunch of twenty-year-olds in it, I learned that I was old.)

When it comes to creativity, the wonderful thing is that everyone does their craft differently. Every creator/teacher's knowledge will be unique and affect us in different ways. I had a teacher in college named Dr. Guy who taught differential equations, and the biggest thing I took from him is that, even if you're over seventy, it's still possible to take the stairs two at a time instead of using the elevator. I used to sit in his office for hours asking more questions about how to stay fit than about my homework. I still got an A, of course.

— — — — — — — — — — — — — — — — —

Name an area in which you'd like to grow creatively.

Do some research and find three classes or organizations
to help you learn about it. Local. Available. Doable.
If not now, when?

— — — — — — — — — — — — — — — — —

Outside of class situations, seeking out meetups, joining alumni associations, applying for apprenticeships (not the Middle Ages kind, where you get sent away as a kid to be an indentured servant, that's probably against child labor laws now)—there are a myriad of avenues available out there to put ourselves in positions where we can work alongside people in creative fields. And the more hands-on we're able to involve ourselves, the better! On-the-job training is the best experience we can get. (That annoying teenaged "I'll-make-mistakes-myself!" attitude is pretty smart. Don't tell them I said that.) Whether painting, crafting, or experimental robot welding, when our bodies are involved in the creative process rather than the theory of it, we learn the most. Just *try* learning Spanish from a book and then attempt to speak it to someone in real life. Do you suddenly feel like an idiot who can't remember the word *enchilada*? Join the club! DOING it is the only way to truly learn. That's why whenever anyone asks me how to get started in show business, I reply, "Don't move to LA. Get experience locally. Get on film sets as an intern, PA, whatever. Watch other people work. Get experience, THEN look outside for more guidance. But seriously, don't move to LA right now. Traffic is already bad enough here as it is."

— — — — — — — — — — — — — — — — — — —

Name mentors in your life who have had a firsthand impact on your creativity. How/where did you meet them? What did they provide that gets you through tough times?

Who is in your life who actively does that NOW? If no one, what is one step you can take to try and find that person?

— — — — — — — — — — — — — — — — — — —

No matter what our creative pursuits are, people around us can always give SOME kind of advice. The wonderful thing about learning is that it's universal. So go ahead and question everyone around you! Uncle Albert runs a shoe store? Sure, he doesn't know anything about ballet. But he knows about feet. That alone could be worth a trip to Starbucks to treat him to a straight coffee—black, six Splendas—and pick his brain. He might talk a wee bit too much about bunions, but it's worth the trade-off. (Maybe. No guarantee.) Bottom line, there is literally no one in existence who has NOTHING to offer us. And if we're considerate of people's time, very few will say, "I'm sorry, I don't have time to answer questions on a topic I, myself, have devoted my life to." Normal humans can't WAIT to talk about something we love. (And ourselves as we relate to it. Salty, but true!)

— — — — — — — — — — — — — — — — —

List ten people in your life who are close enough to you that you could take them to lunch and pick their brains. Think about each one's expertise and, beside their name, write an aspect of their knowledge that could apply to your creative dreams.

Every single person has something to offer your journey, whatever their background. When in doubt, ask the simple question: "What do you think I should know about [their knowledge/experience] that I don't already?" Ignorance is a disease that can only be cured by the knowledge of others.

— — — — — — — — — — — — — — — — —

In a topsy-turvy fashion, mentorship from the opposite direction can be just as fruitful for our creativity. As in US helping OTHER people. Even if we don't feel qualified! The truth is, we're always better at giving advice than taking it. That's because we're trapped inside our own skulls, with all our history and relativism gumming up the works. How many times over coffee do we give our friends insightful, clearly obvious-to-us advice that didn't occur to them even though they're smart and awesome? When we see someone we love get into a relationship and think, *Damn, that's gonna go down in flames, hard.* But they're totally smitten, so you just stand by and be supportive until it crashes like a train wreck. THEN you can say without pissing your friend off, "I always hated her/him." (Yes, I'm talking about you, Kate. That guy was a deadbeat; listen to me next time!)

The act of communicating about our creativity with others can teach US so many new things about our own processes. It's like a jellyfish tank. Jellyfish require a circular flow of water to survive. They can't exist in a regular fish tank. I think this is true of creators too. Unless we are constantly flowing through our own creativity, then through others' and back again, we can't grow to our full potential. Mentors know that. And inside, we do too.

Personally, I love helping produce other people's work. And telling people how to live their lives. (Book in hand = case in point.) Whenever I get stuck on my own work, I deliberately reach out to help another person who's struggling with their creativity. And inevitably I give them advice over coffee that later makes me go, *Oh! That's what I needed to hear myself!* DUH! The mentor/mentee situation is beneficial to both ends! (The mentee/manatee one . . . questionable.) There's no scarcity of knowledge in this world. But there is a scarcity of kindness. And in a karmic way, reaching out to help someone else, even for selfish reasons, truly can mean the world.

I once had Paul Feig, creator of *Freaks and Geeks*, out of the blue send me an email of compliments about *The Guild*. This was probably eight years ago, but to this day, I can't tell you how much that random message lifted me up. If someone I admired THAT much took the time to reach out and send a note, I HAD to be on the right path. (Also, how did he get my email? That part is really weird.) Having that email in my mental back pocket amongst a few other inspiring moments, like when Joss Whedon recently took me to dinner and said, "I believe in you. I just wanted to make sure you knew" <*insert tears*>, helps me beat back the sucking void of depression that often looms in my mind. Those faithful statements give me strength to say, "Nah, you're wrong. I don't suck. Things aren't hopeless. Because you know who disagrees with you, bad thoughts? PAUL FEIG AND JOSS WHEDON! SO SUCK IT!"

— — — — — — — — — — — — — — —

Reach out to someone near you who needs a mentor's boost and offer to take them to lunch. Even if your fields are drastically different, lend them an ear and whatever advice you can give them. Does your generosity help them? How does that feel?

How does the process of helping THEM later help spur your own creativity?

— — — — — — — — — — — — — —

Friends

Finally, let me state the obvious: we're not meant to be solitary creatures. That's for jaguars. And badgers. And moose. If you're not one of those, keep reading. (If you are, grats on literacy.) Just like heroes in books, as creators, we need a set of friends to help us overcome our faults and beat the bad guy in the end. The Harry Potter franchise isn't just about a kid named Harry Potter who defeats Voldemort. It's his journey, sure, hence the title, but Harry succeeds because of the help of Ron and Hermione. (Whom I will never have hooking up in my personal canon. You can't make me. Harrymione4lyfe!) I mean we can TRY to succeed without connecting with other people who are struggling in the creative trenches alongside us, but why? It's so much more fulfilling to suffer with others! That's why I always say to my partner after eating something disgusting, "This is awful! Try it!"

Linking arms with people to help keep our creative goals on track is crucial. Think of it as gathering a "Creative Friend Alliance."

Ugh. That name is terrible. "Friend Coterie"? "Artist Guild"? "Imagination Tribe"? "Creativity Clan"? ⇽ HELL no! Okay, I'll admit it. I'm just flailing around trying to avoid using the phrase *support group*. Yes, it's a bit of a dirty concept for people who sneer at empathy and primarily use internet memes to communicate, but the fact is that humans *need* to be supported. It's how we extend our family outside our gene-stuffs. The concept may have originated with Alcoholic's Anonymous in the 1930s, but I bet they've always existed, back to the beginnings of civilization. Picture a Neanderthal saying to another Neanderthal, "I have this cave painting I'm stuck on. Give me your opinion on it, Glort?"

Many years ago I was invited to join . . . FINE, a "support

group" of women who met weekly to share creative wins in their lives. We were all struggling in show business, and the goal was to help each other be more accountable. While eating pancakes. (I kind of suspect it was inspired by *The Secret*, but I didn't put the group together, so my hands are clean.) The group took me from feeling very alone and helpless to feeling confident and risking more for my creativity. (Also super guilty if I didn't show up with progress every week. Guys, peer pressure is effective!) This accountability was the primary reason I wrote *The Guild* web series instead of playing video games all day for the rest of my life. And writing that show *for sure* changed my life. (FYI, that group was named "Chick-In." Proof that the name is irrelevant as long as the intentions are good!)

So how do we find people to form our own creative support group? Well, for one, start local. We'll never know what dreams the people around us may secretly harbor unless we approach a friend with, "Hey, do you have any creative goals you'd like to achieve this year? Would you like to meet weekly to keep up with them together? No, I'm not trying to draft you into a cult, promise!" This not only gives us a great excuse to hang out with people we like, but it's a wonderful way to connect in a new way and deepen relationships. It's also a way to find out surprising things about those we love. After I expressed an interest in learning a new hobby recently, my brother told me he was learning how to draw with online tutorial courses. I'd had no idea! Cool, bro, I wish you lived closer, I'd join you. Now send your niece a birthday present, NOW!

If we are able to gather a small group of supporters together to hold each other accountable for our creative goals, we can more easily achieve great things! (Or guilt each other when we fall into lazy, slacker behavior. Either/or.)

— — — — — — — — — — — — — — — —

In each board in the scaffolding below, write the names of friends and acquaintances who you could reach out to for support on your creative journey.

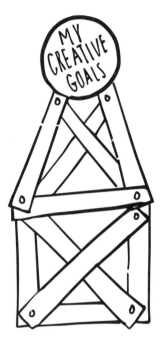

After filling in the names, lean back and take in the new picture. Does your creative journey feel more possible with all this new structural support?

— — — — — — — — — — — — — — — —

What if we can't find immediate friends to join our group? Well, think of areas you have creative interests in and GO THERE. Yes, physically, in person. I know that's a strange concept nowadays, consider me old-fashioned. Think, *Where would someone in my town be if they were trying to learn how to create X?* (Hint: the answer is not the local biker bar unless *X* = trouble.) It could mean tracking down and joining an existing creative support group, or gathering new members by getting out and meeting people through classes or networking events or conventions. Yes, going out is scary. I get it. I rarely leave the house after 5:00 p.m. There are too many shiny lights and stuff at night-night time. But when we put ourselves in situations tied to our creative passions, we're more likely to connect with people we click with. If I bump into another writer at a Hollywood party who loves *The Mighty Boosh*, I know that our creativity will probably align with each other's. I'll put their number in my phone. And then likely be too shy to ever text them. But as we've demonstrated time and time again in this book, DON'T BE LIKE FELICIA IN THIS INSTANCE. THAT'S THE POINT!

If anyone is afraid of the whole "human contact with strangers thing," the internet is only MOSTLY all animated GIFs and alt-right haters. It's also a place that contains cool, interesting people with similar interests. When I started making my web series, I was one of the first out of the gate. But I knew there were others out there too, and I wanted to meet them. So I scoured the web for creators like me. When I found a video I loved, I would send a compliment and share a link to my own work. That simple. Through that process, I became friends with Rachel Bloom, creator of *Crazy Ex-Girlfriend*, and met my friend Ryan Copple, who later became the CEO of my company and business partner, among other things. (I call him Ryco because my brother Ryon is the "official" holder of the name in my life. It's okay to rename your friends, right? As I type this I'm getting self-conscious in a not-good way.)

Rather than having to pick out online collaborators one by one, which granted, might not have a quick success rate, if we're a fan of something, we can also look for places like-minded fans congregate. Within those communities could be the seeds of a formidable creative group. I've had many people tell me they've been inspired by meeting people in chat rooms and forums around my show *The Guild* and my company Geek & Sundry. (I've also had TSA agents tell me they conceived a baby while watching my videos. That one we don't need to talk about further.) The social networking part of the internet is maligned, but even in the face of some of the terrible stuff it's doing to society, I will always think of the internet as a place where people who love things can connect around that love and support each other. If we ignore all the trolls and bots and data-manipulation-by-huge-corporations stuff, it can actually be a great place to meet people!

— — — — — — — — — — — — — — — — —

Brainstorm five ways you could meet people locally to connect with others around one of your creative interests. If it's gaming, look for a local game shop with evening events. If it's meditation, look for a seminar. Comb every resource you can to see where supportive people might be!

Which event or idea excites you most? Which one works, but slightly scares you?

Can you talk yourself into doing the scary one first? *What do you have to lose?*

— — — — — — — — — — — — — — — — —

— — — — — — — — — — — — — — — —

Name some things you are a fan of that align creatively
with what you want to make in the future.

Take one topic and find places online where you could connect
with others about it. Join a forum. Or a chat room.
Or a Facebook group. If someone in the comments seems to share
your creative aspirations, reach out and say something!
You'll never know who might become a potential ally unless
you reach out, online or offline.

— — — — — — — — — — — — — — — —

Creating is hard. It requires hunkering down for grinding work between the sparks of enthusiasm. We all need a Scooby Gang to keep us going. (Of course technically, if you think about it, Scooby isn't really the one who DOES anything in the show. He doesn't solve crimes. He's a dog. It's all about Fred, Daphne, and Velma doing the legwork, and Shaggy and Scooby messing around trying to eat every salami sandwich in sight, while stumbling on a clue here and there. It really should be called the Velma Gang, right? *RIGHT?* Is this the longest parenthetical in the book? Sorry, I just really feel strongly about this issue!)

Our best allies are those who are fascinated by what we have to say. And always want to see more from us. So seek out and gather those troops and hold them close as you embark on your new creative life. The only wrong thing we can do is stay stuck and isolated. Those words are the antithesis of creativity.

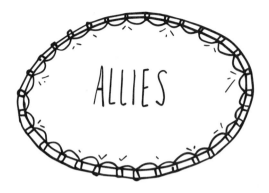

- - - - - - - - - - - - - - - - -

Commit to the idea of forming a creative support group!
Name it and design your own logo.
(Use stickers, clip art, glitter, whatever is fun!)

Pick a date to start. Within a month from now, please!
Decide on a place to meet.
Now . . . send out an invite and make it so!

- - - - - - - - - - - - - - - - -

PLAYTIME!

It's time to _____ with the _____
and harness the joy of _____!

If we were to brainstorm the perfect cliché of "creator," I guarantee we'd come up with a lot of dark clothing, cigarettes, and torment. I had an obsession with black crushed velvet and lace as a teen, partially because of Winona Ryder in *Beetlejuice*, partially because I wanted to look "arty." The sum benefit? A lot of embarrassing pictures I can now Instagram on #ThrowbackThursdays, and a terrible habit of associating agony with creativity.

The myth that we have to suffer to be creative (along with the equally poop-smelly myth of "If I'm not talented, I shouldn't even try") is what holds most of us back. But it's all poppycock! Balderdash! Ganon and Spinach! (That's a play on a David Copperfield phrase and a Legend of Zelda character. Five people got it. Everyone else, move along.)

We've done a lot of soul-searching, confronting mental enemies, and even philosopher name-dropping here and there (let's hope in accurate contexts). But if there's a single solitary thing I'd love for people to take away from this book, it is:

THE HEART
OF CREATIVITY
IS PLAY

COLOR THE ABOVE IN.
THE CRAZIER, THE BETTER!

Playfulness is the root of all creation. All invention. All discovery. There is no reason NOT to feel joyous when we make things. Even when we encounter problems. In fact, WHEN we encounter problems is when we most need to channel playfulness! It's not indulgent to ask ourselves, "How can I solve this in a way that's fun for me?" I promise the answers will always lead to better solutions. And honestly, what is the worst that could happen? The end product will be worse because you didn't suffer? Hit the road, double theoretical negative! Unless you're a Puritan wearing a hair shirt, that attitude sucks, and we don't have to operate this way.

Play and work don't have to be looked at as opposites. It's not an either/or choice. There is as much seriousness as joy in the attitude of children building a block tower. Their work is important to them WHILE they play. And they take it just as seriously as if they were composing a symphony. I suspect that Mozart, age four, didn't stare at the wall while he was writing minuets and groan, "This *Scheisse* is torture." You know that kid worked with joy under his tiny wig. It should be the same for us olds!

When we focus on the opposite of *play* being the words *grind* or *struggle* or, even better, *drudge* (back the garbage truck up on THAT word), we can feel better justified in incorporating it in EVERY-THING. "How can I make this fun for me?" should be the mantra in every creative activity that we do.

— — — — — — — — — — — — — — — — —

Study the lines on your palm and draw them below.
Then try to make recognizable shapes out of them.

This is play. No one's paying you to do this. But did you notice the intense concentration of WORK you had AS you played? There's no reason that spirit can't be channeled into your actual work too!

— — — — — — — — — — — — — — — — —

— — — — — — — — — — — — — — —

Think of a problem you are having right now in your life. On a separate
piece of paper, brainstorm ONLY FUN ways you could solve this problem. For
example, "How am I going to get money to buy a new car next year?" or
"How can I get my cat to stop looking at me like I'm food?"
If you get stuck, close your eyes and drop your pen on the below graphic.
Then try to solve your problem with something
related to the object your pen landed on.
If you aren't having fun writing, TRY SOMETHING ELSE!

It might not 100 percent provide a solution, but doesn't it feel
freeing to know that problem solving doesn't have to be miserable?

— — — — — — — — — — — — — — —

Just as with any other muscle, we have to exercise play or we lose track of it. Like the area under the butt. I never use those muscles, but after I go to dance class? "Ouch, how long have I been sitting on THOSE things?" Challenging our brains in playful ways is necessary for creating. Because a life of doing the same thing over and over, always taking the easiest solution, surrounding ourselves with unchallenging tasks . . . snore. Ah, I'm sorry! Ten years just went by, where are we now?

Yes, I'm saying we need to FORCE ourselves to play! On a regular basis. It is our JOBS. As ADULTS. I'm the worst, right?

So how do we do it?

Well, for starters, we allow ourselves to be bored.

Yup.

It might seem weird to say, "I need to take a break and stare at a wall to be more playful right now." But that's EXACTLY what we need to do sometimes! We live in a world that gives us no chance to give our brains breathing room, outside of sending us nightmares about showing up naked everywhere by accident. They only have a chance to do THAT because we're unconscious. When we're awake and in the driver's seat? Forget independent play, Brain! EAT JUNK FOOD AND LIKE IT!

We never give ourselves a CHANCE to develop playful, magical thoughts, because the second we get downtime, we're scrolling maniacally through people's status updates, liking and retweeting . . . to what end? I mean, I love baby sloth pictures as much as any sentient being, but they're not helping me come up with creative ideas with their cute, stretchy . . . okay, maybe that was a bad analogy, sloths are the best.

I'm certainly in no place to preach about the ills of social media— my career is built on it. (Follow me on Twitter, BTW.) But I do know that the years I invested the most time in my online persona were my least enjoyable creatively. My brain got locked in craving the "hits" of likes and comments and retweets instead of coming up with new ideas. As an all-or-nothing kind of gal, I had to take drastic measures to reset the way I was behaving. (Time Warner is NOT amenable to temporarily cutting off internet service, FYI.)

It was hard, but I noticed that after stints of unplugging, I would start to be inspired again. I began to brainstorm new projects. I spent way less time doing my hair for selfies. I'm not saying everyone needs to go cold turkey from tech in order to give their brains daydreaming R&R. But let's face it: "Eureka!" will never come from reading a Facebook status update. Unless someone literally types in, "Eureka!" In which case, use the smiley face option as a response.

Even simply building in twenty minutes a day to take a walk or gaze at the sunset is sending an invitation to our brains to play. Like dropping our dogs off at the dog park. "Have fun! I won't interrupt. Just let me know what you discover, please. And if you poop, I'll clean it up!" When we give our brains a little room, we'll never know where they may wander. And what they may discover.

We don't have to be completely hands-off, though. While maintaining the freedom to explore, we can start to nudge our attention in certain creative directions. "I really want to learn how to do figure drawing. Let's go to the museum and look at boobs in paintings to see how they evolved over the ages. Fun, artistic, AND scientific!" As long as we maintain the spirit of play in our ventures, we will always find fertile ground.

I took a stand-up class a few years ago and was, naturally, terrified. I'm very good at sharing my opinions from behind a computer screen, but in front of real humans? Possibly fatal. I was delighted to discover that writing stand-up comedy, at the heart of it, is just allowing our brains to look at the world in their unique way and recording those observations. Particularly the snarky ones. It's one of the purest ways to channel our weirdnesses. (And at free open mic nights, where comics try out new material . . . it's definitely possible to see a LOT of weirdness.) When I forced myself for a few months to walk through the day, pen and tablet in hand, I was astonished at how much my brain actually produced. Especially with the snark. How the material was received is irrelevant. (They laughed. Generally.) But mostly I was just struck by how much potential creativity we all leave on the table by not giving our brains room enough stretch.

OH! WAS THAT A NEW IDEA OR DID I JUST PULL A MUSCLE?

— — — — — — — — — — — —

Take a day and embrace boredom. Every time you reach for your phone, stare at a tree instead. Let your brain sit in idle whenever you can. It's only one day, you can do it! Write down whatever occurs to you throughout that day. Any weird thought that separates you from the mainstream. Anything that makes you smile.

Think about it: all of the above is just a fraction of the creativity you could have if you gave yourself a DAILY dream break!

— — — — — — — — — — — —

In essence, play is the fuel that gets us out of our comfort zones and into the unknown with minimal scariness. Yes, we have to "go to there" in order to be creative. But why use force when we can samba? I've taken improv comedy classes on and off for over a decade. I do it because it helps me be in the present moment, relaxing and reacting, with no plan in hand. (Which is very hard for a savant-level control freak like me.) Minutes on stage feel like HOURS when it doesn't go well. And often it doesn't. But when the magic happens, it's surreal to have something come out of my mouth I never knew I had in me. "Who's in there, and *why is she so relaxed and funny*?" It's freaky and awesome. And shows me that, with the right attitude, we can tap into so many unexpected thoughts and dreams. I hate to introduce the douchey word *gamify* into the book, but wherever you can infuse gameplay in your life? Do it!

Drive home a different way every day. Secretly wear weird underwear with unicorns on it. "Why does Bill have that odd smile on his face today?" Challenging ourselves in big ways and small to play with the world can only yield more creativity. "I challenge myself to get that can of soup from the cupboard before the refrigerator door shuts! I win . . . *nothing! But I won!*" There are infinite sandboxes we can play in!

— — — — — — — — — — — — — — — —

Go to the mall and make up a game for yourself to play there. For example:

- Count how many people wearing band T-shirts you can find in an hour.
- Shop for the outfit you'd wear on a date with your fave movie star.
- Spot five people who could secretly be spies and/or ninjas.
- Browse the makeup store for the name of a potential cartoon nemesis ("Hex Appeal," anyone?).

    The only requirement is to come up with a game
    that makes you wear a secret smile while you do it!

— — — — — — — — — — — — — — — —

— — — — — — — — — — — — — — — — —

Pick an object in the room with you. Describe below as many uses
for the object as you can think of, other than the uses for
which it's intended. The more ridiculous, the better.
Then name ten things that it would NOT be useful for.
Again with the ridiculous thing!

— — — — — — — — — — — — — — — — —

Write an online dating profile for your pet in the first person.
But make them someone NO ONE would want to date.

— — — — — — — — — — — — — — — — —

— — — — — — — — — — — — — — — — —

Imagine you're a time traveler.
Where would you go first?

Where would you NEVER go?

What would you bring with you?

What might you encounter that would
surprise you in a good way? In a bad way?

What's the one object you would steal?

Who would you take a selfie with?

— — — — — — — — — — — — — — — —

It's counterintuitive, but something as simple as narrowing our choices can activate a feeling of play in an amazing way. It's what I love about writing comic books. It's a very restrictive format. There are a set number of pages, only so much space per page, and no room for too much talking. (But lots of explosions and hidden identities!) It's almost easier to be innovative when we have to work within strict limitations. That's why the TV show *Chopped* is so satisfying. They don't offer the chefs the whole pantry; they give them jackfruit and pig's feet and expect them to make magic. It's amazing what people come up with. And it's surprising that, however good a chef someone is, they'll absolutely never in a million years make me want to eat pig's feet.

Look up from this book, name the first object you
see in the room, and write it below.

Now write a title of a movie with that word
in the following genres:

Western:

Action:

Horror:

Romance:

Fantasy:

Science Fiction:

Oscar-Worthy Drama:

Slogan for Dish Soap:

Write a story starting each sentence with a different letter of the alphabet.

A

B

C

D

E

F

G

H

I

J

k

L

M

N

O

P

Q

R

S

T

U

V

W

X

Y

Z

Brainstorm ten new dishes based on your favorite ingredient.

Which sounds the tastiest to you?
Why not give it a shot? There's always takeout if it fails!

Fill in the dialogue below. Give yourself a five-minute timer.

Congratulations. You just made a comic!

When we make a habit of living our lives with a playful attitude, we can be secure in knowing that we have a tiny SPARK kindled inside us (one that we can rev like an engine) to get us over and through the bumps we encounter in our creative projects. Because however satisfying it is to challenge ourselves with "Make a list of everything that's yellow!" we all probably want to build toward something bigger. Whether it's sewing a quilt for your mom's birthday or making a movie in our backyard on our iPhone, we can choose to treat any act of creativity like a maze. When we reach a dead end we can either A) try to bash the wall in front of us with our head to get through, or B) say, "That didn't work. But that looks like a fun way to try over there!" I have done a LOT of head bashing in my day.

But what if we have a vague idea of a bigger creative project but don't even know where to start?

Well, we can use others' work to give us a playful boost! No, I'm not encouraging plagiarism; please don't go write a script called *Star Tracks* and tell the lawyers I said it was okay. But in order to spark play, we can use other people's work as a springboard, to whatever degree we need to feel joy while creating. Training wheels aren't for sissies, they're for EVERYONE. (My grandpa told me that at age six and he was right!)

From reading a dozen Westerns for research because we want to tell a story with someone in a cowboy hat but don't know where to start, all the way to something more direct, like using the characters of Harry Potter to make hand puppets, or painting fan art dedicated to *Breaking Bad* (cool meth lab, bro!). If someone else's work helps us get in touch with our inner sense of play, there isn't a moment wasted in our using it to PRACTICE.

Without my love of games, I wouldn't have created any of the web series I did. Gaming was an inspiration that gave me a jumping-off point to get into filmmaking. I'm GRATEFUL for it! It's similar to why coloring books are so satisfying. We're given a head start with the underlying drawing to fill in something unique to us. There is no embarrassment in enjoying them. Hell, I'll do it in public. With crayons.

I can't tell you how irritated I get when people sneer at fan art and fan fiction, or put down someone's creativity because it's "derivative." In more high-brow galleries, there have been whole art exhibits dedicated to the works Picasso inspired. The director Quentin Tarantino is famous for inserting shot-for-shot homages to old movies he loves in his own. In my opinion, homage/fanfic? They're just cousins who can't marry legally because they're a little too close. It's all a question of degree. If *Buffy* inspires someone to write a book series about a woman who stabs things . . . in my opinion, there can never be enough lady-stabbing, so have at it!

Tweak a recipe! Rewrite a famous poem for fun! Try on different creativity and see how it fits! We don't always need to start with a blank bolt of cloth and make an outfit from scratch. We may only be ready to decorate an existing jacket with a fancy pin at first. But if we do THAT enough times, we may be able to build up the confidence one day to rip it into pieces and remake it completely into a dress. Or a jumpsuit. That style is in, but it makes me look stubby, so I'm a pass, but you do you, dude.

Whatever degree allows us the most fun is the RIGHT degree. Bottom line, we'll never know if a creative area is a place we want to play unless we try!

Draw in weird expressions on the faces below.

In the empty space, draw your own figure from
scratch in the style of the others.
Use inspiration wherever you can find it to start creating!

You win a vacation to go inside your favorite fictional
world. What is the world and what do you do there? Do you
encounter some of the characters from the original creation?
Write what could happen below when you interact!

Find a painting you love. Draw your own version in the first box. Then
do a copy of your copy. And then a copy of a copy of a copy.

Do you see how your own identity comes out as you
get further and further from the source?

_ _ _ _ _ _ _ _ _ _ _ _ _ _ _ _ _ _

Take a song you love and rewrite one stanza of the lyrics.

Now make up a slightly different melody to go with it.

Then make it more different. Then more different.

At what point does the song start to become yours more than theirs?

_ _ _ _ _ _ _ _ _ _ _ _ _ _ _ _ _

One of the most successful pieces of content I've ever made was the music video "Do You Want to Date My Avatar." It has almost thirty million hits on YouTube. (Not as many as "Baby Shark," but respectable.) The reason I wrote it? I was bored one day and, for fun, I made a playlist of all the cheesy dance songs that made me happy when I was procrastinating from my "real" work. Then I thought, *I can do this myself!* I studied probably thirty of them (DANCE PARTY!) and then wrote my own version. On a lark. But it turned into something more. Because I had so much fun with it, I was sure other people would too. And they did! My outfit from that video is now in the Smithsonian American History Collection. It feels pretentious to even type that, sorry, but it's true!

We can never tell what the result of our creative ventures will be. But if we feel that sense of play while we work, we can always rest assured that whatever direction we go is the right one for us. So when in doubt, ask, "What would a clown do?"

Actually, please don't. Stephen King does that. It's the stuff of nightmares. Let me rephrase: Look at any problem as an opportunity to play.

WHAT WOULD A CLOWN DO?

What is *that?* I literally said DON'T do the clown question! Ugh! My illustrator has gone rogue. Oh well. At least they seem to have fun. Drawing a clown. <*shudder*>

I'm going to go shower now.

Oh God, the clown is in the shower with me!

Help!

7

QUESTS

It's time to gather what we've learned about ourselves and set out on an epic journey toward a more creativity-filled life. WOOT! FOREVER ROAD TRIP!

‒ ‒ ‒ ‒ ‒ ‒ ‒ ‒ ‒ ‒ ‒ ‒ ‒ ‒ ‒

Write ten words below describing how you feel about "creativity."

Now compare what you wrote to the list you made on page 17. Is there more positivity? More hope? Less "blah"? Great!

‒ ‒ ‒ ‒ ‒ ‒ ‒ ‒ ‒ ‒ ‒ ‒ ‒ ‒ ‒

Our creative makeover is almost finished. We look fabulous and are ready to attend the ball/rave/Lovecraftian portal-opening party/ etc.! Head-to-toe *buffed*. We. Look. Gooooood!

Um . . . where do we go from here?

Hark! A Quest!

Rather, several of them. That will never end.

I'm scaring everyone, aren't I? Let's reset.

We've done a deep dive into ourselves. We have the tools to get our voices out in the world that we didn't have before. We've faced our fears and can brandish our weirdness with pride.

So what quests can we embark on to make sure we don't forget everything we just learned? Like when I swear off carbs, then eight hours later I'm stuffing a baguette in my mouth.

Make Room

It would be great if, after reading this book, we were all so taken by creative urges that we spent every spare minute working on them. But that's probably unrealistic and/or unsustainable and/or border-line obsessive. (Kudos to obsessives, though. I ate oatmeal every morning for two years once. It was good for my colon and probably not much else.)

Most of us have full-time jobs and can't quit to start leatherworking for a living. There are children and pets to feed, so forget sailing around the world in a self-built pirate ship for now. As we age, we become overburdened by obligations. Our Facebook feed epitomizes this. I mean, how often do we actually talk to that person from college who posts dozens of updates about their cat every day? We don't CARE about Casey McWhiskers, but we can't seem to bring ourselves to unfollow. In the face of all that, how can we add creativity and personal growth to our schedules? *How is this going to work? Does Kohl's have a special on space/time pockets we can escape into?*

Everything we do is wrapped up in a series of checks and balances of our time. And one second spent on something we don't like is a second away from something we'd love.

Yes, bills need to get paid, families fed, but it's also necessary to be vigilant about our need to create. Like any garden, our lives become overgrown. We need to take time to trim back and make room. For the army of garden gnomes who will come alive in our hour of need if there's a magical apocalypse . . . wait, what? Uh . . . like I said, trim back and make room! Forget everything I said after that.

— — — — — — — — — — — — — — — — — — —

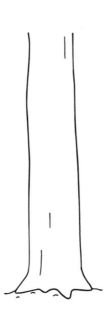

Picture yourself as a tree. Write what is most important to you in the trunk area. What you can't live without. Now start drawing branches and on each one of them, write something that takes your attention away from the trunk. Jobs. Hobbies. Nonessential relationships. Social media. Chores. Make a branch for everything that takes up your time and clutters your life. See all the things that are draining your roots? It would make any real tree topple! Your branches have to be pruned in order to make room for your new, more creative Hero-Self. So let's make another tree.

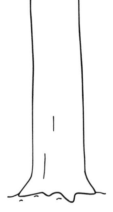

In the trunk, write your life essentials again. Then start
drawing branches, but only include things that are a priority
for you. That enrich your life. Include the kinds of creativity
you want to prioritize. The more specific, the better.

Compare the two trees. What's missing?

Now you know areas that need to be minimized or lopped from your
life in order to make you freer to create. If there aren't enough
differences, don't worry! Trimming trees too drastically can harm
the trunk. (I say that with all the authority of someone who
doesn't know anything about arboriculture.) ANY trimming can allow
you a little room. And all you need is a little to make progress.

Nothing is written in one fell swoop. This book was typed letter by letter. No matter what we have to deal with in our lives, we can keep moving toward our creative goals as long as we keep *pushing forward*. Just push it. Push it, real good. *<snicker> <back to serious>* Just as our attention is finite, our time is finite too. It's our fuel. And we don't want to run out before we . . . er, let's not talk about death stuff. But truly, what we spend our time on *is* our lives.

— — — — — — — — — — — — — — — — —

What could you do for thirty minutes a day that would help you accomplish a larger creative goal? Fifteen minutes? Five minutes? Two?

Pick a length of time to commit to and start today. Right now. This book can count, that's fine. I'll give hall passes for that one.

— — — — — — — — — — — — — — — — —

Remember, our job with our creativity is not to produce something for others to consume. That's a side benefit IF we choose to share it when we're done. Our job is to show up, put the time in, and finish things. To live fully creative lives and share our weirdness in a way only WE can. If we keep showing up, IT will show up. In a lovely way, our very presence expresses an important faith in ourselves. Like, when our dads show up to our dance recital, it means something, right? So let's channel a little Dad for ourselves and our creativity!

We have finite energy but infinite potential. If we can commit to just one page a day. One photo a day. One stitch a day. One teeny-tiny portion of time EACH DAY toward our creative goals, we can work toward achieving a dream. In the end, only zero will give us nothing to build on. But SOMETHING will always add up to something. That's an unintimidating math fact.

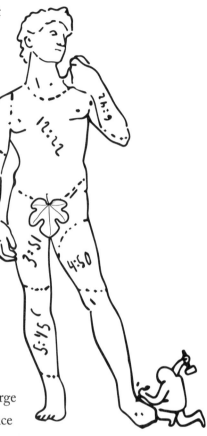

Keep Exploring!

It's strange to think that large swaths of the Earth were once mysterious, uncharted territory.

Like, if we set out on a ship somewhere, we'd breach the very border of our own existence and encounter societies we'd never dreamed of. (And probably wipe out those societies with a sneeze. No, I'm not using genocide as punch line, it's just the downer truth.) But having now explored the whole Earth doesn't mean we know everything about it. That goes for who we are inside too.

Write everything about yourself inside the paper doll below. Adjectives, nouns, verbs, doodles—whatever comes to mind. Especially include the new things you've discovered on your journey through this book.

This is your new Hero-Self. *Hot, right?* We've added so much on this journey! Pat that paper doll on the back!

BUT (sigh, there's always a "but") just because we've deepened our knowledge of ourselves doesn't mean we know everything. We will never know all we can be. Sorry, we are just as unexplored and fascinating and mysterious as the Earth once was. Our boundaries will never limit us, because we have infinite depth.

Like those sequences on police shows where the team looks at a surveillance photo and says, "Enhance, enhance, enhance!" we always have the ability to uncover more of who we are and add to what we know about ourselves. We just need to activate those new things by constantly EXPOSING ourselves to new things.

So take on the challenge of doing just that! Follow rabbit holes of interest as deep as they'll go. Go on a trip somewhere new, even if it's just somewhere local. Say yes to everything (legal), even if it's scary. It is not self-indulgent to devote time to studying something fascinating *just because*. That's how we grow ourselves. Yesterday I didn't know what an axolotl was even though I pretended that I did in conversation. I went home and looked it up. Now I know. It's an adorable amphibian that is a weird phallic shape with a fancy ruffle. Now *everyone* knows!

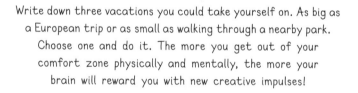

YOU'RE WELCOME

— — — — — — — — — — — — — —

Write down three vacations you could take yourself on. As big as a European trip or as small as walking through a nearby park. Choose one and do it. The more you get out of your comfort zone physically and mentally, the more your brain will reward you with new creative impulses!

— — — — — — — — — — — — — —

--- --- — ---- -- — ----- —

Draw a rabbit hole below and write a subject in it.
The first thing that comes to mind.

Now spend thirty minutes on the internet following the trail
of this subject. Go from Wikipedia entry to blog post to YouTube
video and back again, clicking or searching on whatever you come
across that interests you. Follow your curiosity.
Where do you end up?

What is one thing you've learned that you want to remember?

You never know where wandering may take you in life,
and that's the point!

-- --- ------ -- ----- —

— — – — — — – — — – — — — – — —

List as many things as you can think of to finish this statement:
I wish I understood _ _ _ _ _ _ _ _ more.

Your curiosity is an arrow that will lead you to discover new parts of
yourself. So whenever you can, pull that arrow back and let it fly!

— — – — — — – — — – — — — – — —

To continue to grow our Hero-Selves, we have to keep pushing
the boundaries of our comfort zones. There's a tendency to pay attention only to things that AGREE with us. That make us feel GOOD.
But inner growth is spurred by all sorts of things: joy, grief, discomfort, and mistakes too. Exposing ourselves to radically different
subjects can broaden our minds in unexpected ways. Why not pick
a subject that's completely unappealing on the face of it and read a
book on it? Ask a friend about something that normally makes your
eyes glaze over when they talk about it, and try to learn why they love
it so much. For me, the person and subject are clear: Wil Wheaton
and hockey. The idea of asking him what a "hat trick" is and trying to
focus on his answer is making me doze off just thinking about it, but
for the sake of my personal growth I'll fall on that sword. On social
media, include new accounts about things you don't normally see
in your feeds. (*Cheerleader Weekly* sub, anyone?) We can never know
when a chance encounter might inspire us to go in a new creative
direction. "Trapeze school? Twenty feet off the ground? You've got
to be . . . WHEEE!! Where's the circus? Hire meeeeee!"

Bottom line, be willing to get uncomfortable to get more
complicated.

‒ ‒ ‒ ‒ ‒ ‒ ‒ ‒ ‒ ‒ ‒ ‒ ‒ ‒

Name a subject you've never wanted to know about.

Find ONE fact about it that makes it interesting to you. What is it?

See? You would never have known that fact if you hadn't forced
yourself out of your comfort zone. Congrats! Now you never
have to study that subject again if you don't want to!

‒ ‒ ‒ ‒ ‒ ‒ ‒ ‒ ‒ ‒ ‒ ‒ ‒ ‒

The last part of this "Keep Exploring!" quest is trying to make a
HABIT of exploring our own creativity. If every day we acknowledge
with our actions "I'm a creative person!" we train our bodies to fall
into creative patterns as we go through life. Eventually they become
unconscious and we don't have to think about them. We brush our
teeth every morning without thinking, *Oh, I should brush my teeth*,
right? (I hope.) Why not make creativity a habit too?

Whether we pledge to write in a journal every morning, or free-
style rap to our fish every time we feed it, in making a habit of being
creative in small ways, we are priming ourselves to be READY TO
WORK when we turn our eye toward bigger creative goals. A ballet
dancer doesn't perform in front of an audience without practicing
at the barre beforehand, right? Our creative muscle is just that: a
muscle. Exercise it regularly and it'll be there when we tackle the big
stuff. None of that effort is a WASTE! It's all enriching the soil for
when we plant that bigger creative seed we desperately want to grow.
So that eventually we get to gobble up the yummy-ass fruit. (After
we wash off whatever pollution the world throws on it. Or just buy
organic. Except for avocados and bananas, they're safe to buy the
regular version of . . . I'm stopping now.)

Forming a creative habit encourages us to collect all our weird and wonderful thoughts on a regular basis, which is crucial. Because if we don't collect them when they occur to us, the winds of memory will scatter them away, and we'll never find them again. Which sucks, because we are worth collecting! We all need to be hoarders of our own brilliance! Yes, we can also say our thoughts are brilliant—that's okay too!

> Sidenote: If we feel shame or embarrassed about telling our-selves that we're brilliant, let me just pull the car over and say something: calling ourselves brilliant does not make us think we're better than anyone else. It's other people who make our own love of ourselves about THEM. Their disdain of us has nothing to do with us, really. It has everything to do with their not believing THEY are brilliant.
>
> ## THEY ARE BRILLIANT TOO. WE CAN ALL SHINE WITHOUT DIMMING EACH OTHER'S LIGHTS!
>
> /endsidenote /endquest

How could you regularly practice creativity in a small way? What seems fun? Some examples:

Keep a dream journal.

Instagram your breakfast every morning.

Learn song lyrics in the shower.

Challenge yourself to come up with one new idea a day.

Whatever you pick, try to tie it to something you already do.
If it becomes something that's already a part of your life,
it will be easier to remember to get it done regularly!

Commit and Finish

At this point, we're awash in the potential of our creativity. We've made room. We're developing habits. Possibility is drenching us in the feel-goods and the "I-can-do-its." This is GREAT! Let's gather our treasures in the exercise below, just to see what we've uncovered.

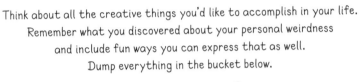

Think about all the creative things you'd like to accomplish in your life.
Remember what you discovered about your personal weirdness
and include fun ways you can express that as well.
Dump everything in the bucket below.

I guarantee this is a big list. Which is entirely NOT doable at once. Yay! As someone who fills four plates at a Vegas buffet and eats exactly two shrimp cocktails and a rice pudding in the end, I feel you. Our creative eyes are always bigger than our creative mouths. In order to take all the lessons of this book and carry them forward, we must focus. Okay, yes, we COULD just finish the book and walk around with that classic self-help afterglow without acting on it, but that feeling lasts maaaaaaaaybe a month. Then, like a sachet in your underwear drawer, it fades and we're left with a packet of dead leaves. So let's actually DO something with our creativity, cool? By focusing on *one goal at a time.*

What bucket-list item is your biggest creative priority right
now? It can be as small as redecorating your room or as big
as renovating the ruin of an entire medieval Italian village by hand.
(Good luck with that. Seriously. And invite me when it's done.)
Whatever you want to devote your creative energy to NOW, write
it down at the top of the ladder below. Then spell out the steps in the
ladder rungs you could take to achieve this bigger creative goal. Make
sure every step is possible as a result of your OWN hard work. If you feel
stress while thinking about moving from one rung to the next, add a rung.
The goal is to make this process as granular and actionable as possible.

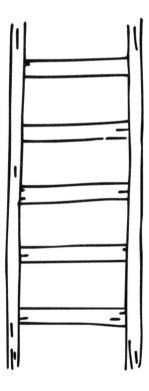

Great! This is your next project after finishing this book!

Creative commitment made! Exciting? Nerve-wracking? Did it make everyone sweat a bit? Of course. But we will never get anywhere if we don't focus on one thing at a time. And then <u>see that thing through before moving on!</u> ↞▨

UNDERLINING THINGS IS WHEN I USE MY MOM VOICE.

It is so easy to flit through life like a creative magpie, chasing one shiny object after another. Even when we commit to one specific goal, like "I want to create a scrapbook filled with pictures of my dog Snuffy!" it's so easy to fail to see that commitment through. Because when we're struggling at the midpoint and lose confidence in our vision, or our anxiety kicks in about the end results, the easiest thing to think is, *That* NEW *idea I had in the shower seems* SO MUCH BETTER AND EASIER. *And Snuffy pooped on the floor yesterday so he's in the dog house. Literally. So let's jump ship for that other thing instead!* In internet meme language:

This is understandable and totally unproductive. It's like allowing ourselves to eat cotton candy for lunch every day and then wondering why we have no teeth left. We cannot improve as creators until we see things through. So go ahead and jot down that new idea for later, but then go back to the old one and COMPLETE IT. That's how we get better. That's how we create proof that we've lived. It's the amber that traps our creativity and gives us a teeny slice of immortality. I'm passionate about this because I am talking to myself here. FINISH THINGS, FELICIA! YOU HAVE NO MORE ROOM IN THE STORAGE UNIT FOR HALF-DONE PROJECTS!

New ideas seem so much more attractive because when we come up with them, we're picturing them complete and perfect. But they're a lie. They don't actually exist. We're delusional at that point. Second date, "I want to breathe your skin every day" infatuated. How can a relationship that's old enough that we keep the bathroom door open when we poop survive THAT feeling?

By digging in and making it legal.

— — — — — — — — — — — — — — — — — —

Below, write a contract with yourself naming a creative goal and pledging to see it through. Throw in legalese if you know it, make it up if you don't. Everyone has seen enough lawyer shows, you can do it. Go on to the next page if you need more room.

Sign it. Have a friend witness it. Notarize it if you are
really thorough. This is your commitment.
Not legally binding. But MORALLY binding. With me.

— — — — — — — — — — — — — — — — —

Bottom line, I believe that in each and every person there's a unique, imaginative creator just waiting to lend their voice to the world. And I am urging everyone to find the strength to channel that creativity into whatever format they choose, and see it through.

Alas, I can't be in each of my reader's houses whispering encouragement/threats while they create. (I'd love to find a way make it happen, though. Maybe I can record phrases like "You can do it!" "You go, person!" "Stop watching TV and DO something!" in a kind of naggy, non-relaxing meditation tape? I'll look into it.) I do know that it's a rare person who can persist completely alone. We have to surround ourselves with supportive voices who hold our feet to the fire.

So gather those role models, mentors, and friends. Use any of their strengths to help see this first creative commitment through. We can rely on them, if only to guilt us into keeping going. Blackmail? Extortion? Whatever it takes, have them help you get this thing done!

— — — — — — — — — — — — — — —

Write one person in each category who could help you keep
climbing your creative goal ladder. Specify how they can help
you achieve your goal going forward.

Role Model:

Mentor:

Friend:

Reach out and text or email the Mentor and Friend RIGHT NOW.
Yes, I'm putting you on the spot! Declare your creative goal to them
and ask them if they'd be willing to support you on your quest.
If not, scratch them out and move on to someone else.
For the Role Model, write a physical letter to
them and put it in your dream file.

Your intentions are out in the world now. They exist
and are supported. There is no shame in needing a
companion's help on the lonely road of creation!

— — — — — — — — — — — — — — —

It's such a monumental achievement to actually FINISH something. And no matter how long it may take us to climb our creative
ladders, we all have the tools to do it. We have the motivation. We
have the help. And when we finish . . . there is always the next ladder just WAITING for us! Which is sure to be just as frustrating and
rewarding to climb as the last, but shh, ignore that and start climbing.

How good does having a creative plan feel? Like a self-made syllabus for a class we can't be graded in. Being homeschooled is great!

Never Give Up

There is no doubt that enemies will rear their ugly, malformed heads along whatever creative path we choose. But if we have our eyes out for them, they can't sneak up on us. We've prepared! We've overcome our fears! We have weapons! Not illegal or pointy ones, but weapons nonetheless!

We WILL reach our creative goals if we persist. Stay focused. Look to allies for support. And use the tools in this book to cut off enemies when they start to spring up with their cheery, "Heyo! Care to hear how much you suck?" voices.

— — — — — — — — — — — — — — — —

In the eyes below, write the three biggest enemies to your creativity that you've uncovered during the process of reading this book.

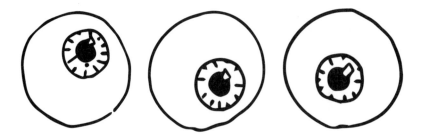

Now write "I have my eye on you" below each eye. You are watching. You are waiting. If you have three eyeballs, you probably feel very secure right now. People with two eyeballs, just know you'll have to multitask.

— — — — — — — — — — — — — — — —

As an even more inspiring "Never Give Up" message, the following may sound a bit woo-woo but I need to include it anyway. (We've all gotten our eye rolls out a long time ago, right?) I believe that when we are clear with our creative intentions, the world lends itself to our cause. And a little bit of Kismet enters our life. No, I'm not saying that when we really want things they just HAPPEN. (If that were possible, I'd have a talking tiny dragon named Julius perching on the end of my finger right now.) But in the same way that when we buy a red car, we see red cars everywhere, if we focus on a specific creative goal, we will start to see the presence of opportunity around that goal in ways that will surprise us.

If we focus on gardening, a beautiful flower in a park could inspire what we grow. If we want to make scarves, a post on Nextdoor forming a local crafting circle might draw our eye. When we hear mention of creative opportunities, they'll no longer pass by unnoticed because we are aware of what we WANT.

If we gather our intentions and stay focused about the importance of creativity in our lives, we'll be surprised how many paths will open up for us and support our dreams.

And finally, when we are challenged or set back or even defeated, there is always one question we can ask ourselves to inspire us to keep going and never give up:

What do I want to have accomplished before I leave this Earth? What would I regret not working harder on? Embracing more? Spending more time on or with?

I know this is four questions. Shut up.

I've read a lot of theoretical physics recently, because if I read things that have no tension and lean toward the snore-worthy, I'm able to sleep better. (Although reading that our universe is guaranteed to implode in, oh, 300 billion years kept me nice and awake for several days.) Something I found eye-opening is that everything that exists now will ALWAYS exist. We are literally all made of stardust.

(And not just because that Joni Mitchell song told us so.) Everything on our planet comes directly from the heart of a star, created after the Big Bang. And whatever exists now, on an atomic level, will always exist. Meaning that the atoms we're made up of will pass into something else after we're gone. It's just science. Therefore, we never TRULY die. It's maybe not reincarnation exactly, but a *continuance* of a sort? Yes. That fact reassured me.

Kind of.

Except then I realized, I won't be aware of becoming part of a worm or a tree or the lettuce inside someone's burrito, so I'd better make the most of my sentience now. (Take it from a seasoned neurotic, trying to head off regret is pretty good motivation.)

The hard truth is, we are finite. And our lives COULD be summarized in a single spreadsheet with tabs like "Number of times we drove our car. Number of TV shows we watched. Number of dinners we had with our friends. Number of bills we forgot to pay that helped ruin our credit ratings." (Thank goodness no one's job is death actuary. Oh wait, it is? Ugh.) We all need to make sure our theoretical spreadsheets include columns for everything important that we want to accomplish in our lifetimes. And that includes creativity.

— — — — — — — — — — — — — — —

Write your dream obituary. What do you want to have accomplished by the time you die? Continue on another sheet of paper if you run out of room.

Does anything you write scream out with urgency, *"Start me now!"*?

— — — — — — — — — — — — — — —

Personally, I'd be disappointed if my own obituary didn't include the amount of time I helped other people, whether through charity or building community. I'd be sad if I never learned another language or wrote a novel or learned how to swim at some point in my life. (I know, I know. Stop nagging me!) We should always think about how we could add numbers to our spreadsheet columns that in the end we would regret never having added. (To be clear: *our* end.)

I know what everyone's thinking. "Gee, thanks for ending this uplifting book on creativity with dire thoughts of mortality." Sorry, but sometimes tough love is motivating!

Seriously, I'm sorry! Here's a picture of a puppy! ON YOUR GRAVE. BUT STILL—A PUPPY!

It's so hard to be persistent when we invest in things that are intangible. If we spend a ton of effort on our careers? We get bonuses. We get compliments. We get money and validation. Spend effort on things like family, children, self-care, or creativity? We may get ups in the long term. But they come with a lot of downs, especially in the short term. And *rarely* do we get any financial or external rewards for them. But in the very end . . . these are the things we will treasure most. And reap the most rewards from.

We don't have a RIGHT to succeed in life. But we do have every right to TRY. So prioritize creativity. Make it a habit. And keep going.

No one is going to rescue us in this world. We have to insist on how awesome we are and keep trying to show people until they frickin' listen! With effort and time, who knows what each of us could accomplish?

But we have to start in order to find out.

GOOD LUCK! GO FORTH! MAKE THINGS! BYEEE!

Group huddle! I'm about to say some stuff that's too earnest, so hold your butts.

We've traveled together a great distance. And discovered that our differences are our greatest assets. We've built ourselves anew as creative, beautiful creatures. However you want to picture that. (Mine has rainbow wings and a laser horn.) We have creative goals we'd like to achieve. We can see them on the horizon and are ready to set out in pursuit of them. Big or small, we have our shoes on and are ready to walk the walk. BONUS: We have the tools to persist, even when buffeted by crappy little winds of strife.

All right, baby birds.

Safe journeys.

It's time to fly. ←

I ACTUALLY TEARED UP WRITING THAT

Every day we have a choice about how to approach the act of living. Whether to take the creative path. Or let our Hero-Selves shine. Or choose *play* rather than *grind*.

There are so many wondrous ways to show our weird to the world.

There is no right or wrong.

Except not to choose.

So . . .

MAKE MISTAKES!
BE CURIOUS!
ASK WHY!
ACCEPT DIFFERENCES!
TRY EVERYTHING!
FOLLOW YOUR JOY!
CREATE FOR NO REASON!
LOVE WHAT YOU ARE!
EMBRACE YOUR WEIRD!

What we've uncovered in this book is just the start. We are like a clam with a new kernel of sand. Yum, gritty! Now we can work on making that sand into a pearl using focus, dedication, and our entire souls. (That's all.) We may not be rewarded in any way but with the gratification of the work itself. *That is enough.* To spend our minutes, hours, and years on something that absorbs us is a gift that is irreplaceable. Priceless. Just like that credit card ad. Except there's no stupid interest.

The truth is, we have uncovered our creative POWER. Yes, it's POWER! It is strong. It is formidable. Probably illegal on some planets. And it is entirely UNIQUE TO US AND THEREFORE SPECIAL. We can own that one hundred percent. (We can also automatically tell haters to "Suck it!" We can own that one hundred percent too.)

Locked. Loaded. Let's do this!

Except one last thing wait sorry.

— — — — — — — — — — — — — — — — —

Let's close the oovy-groovy circle with one last exercise and write, "I am the greatest thing since *Swiss* cheese!" over and over again on this page.

— — — — — — — — — — — — — —

Did that feel different compared to when you wrote it in the beginning of the book? Did you wince less before diving in? Do you now truly believe you are cheesy in new and weirdly wonderful ways?

I believe you are. And hope you do too.

xoxox

Felicia

Oh wait! I figured out how to make those cards from page 92. Clip this out and put it in your wallet. You're welcome!

ACKNOWLEDGMENTS

Copious thanks to the myriad of people who made this book possible. To my fabulous editor, Lauren Spiegel, who filled our phone calls with as many *Game of Thrones* discussions as actual work. To Paul Nielsen, Emily Armstrong, and Spencer Fuller at Faceout Studios, who made the pictures in my head come to life in ways I couldn't imagine. To my copyeditor, Peg Haller, who made me LOL with her Urban Dictionary references in the edit comments. To everyone at S&S, including Jen Bergstrom, Aimée Bell, Jen Long, Jen Robinson, Jessica Roth, Rebecca Strobel, Caroline Pallotta, Sherry Wasserman, Mike Kwan, Jaime Putorti, Abby Zidle, and LJ Jackson, who ensured that this book would be made beautifully and reach the right audience's hands. To my fabulous agent, Erin Malone, without whom I wouldn't bother writing books, I'd just stay home and play video games and be sad about my laziness. To my mom; my dad; my brother, Ryon; my work-wife Ryan Copple. To Amy Phillips, who takes such good care of my baby that I can feel less guilty about working so much. To my partner who, after reading a draft of this book, said, "This is so helpful. You really need to read your own book!" To the fans on my Discord and Twitch channels, who keep me company in the online world. And, finally, to everyone who read my memoir and told me it inspired them to create something: this book wouldn't exist without you. You showed me the joy of helping people through art. You inspired me to create. I can't wait to see what you make yourselves!

MORE BOOKS FOR YOUR CREATIVE JOURNEY

If You Want to Write by Brenda Ueland
Syllabus by Lynda Barry
The Artist's Way by Julia Cameron
How to Be an Explorer of the World by Keri Smith
Bird by Bird by Anne Lamott
Steal Like an Artist by Austin Kleon
The Life-Changing Magic of Tidying Up by Marie Kondo
The Creative Habit by Twyla Tharp

And lastly . . . go create!

ABOUT THE AUTHOR

Felicia Day is the *New York Times* bestselling author of *You're Never Weird on the Internet (Almost)* and a professional actor. She has appeared in numerous films and television shows, such as *Supernatural*, *The Magicians*, and *Mystery Science Theater 3000*. Felicia is best known for her work in the web video world, behind and in front of the camera. She costarred in Joss Whedon's internet musical *Dr. Horrible's Sing-Along Blog*, which won an Emmy in 2009. She also created and starred in the seminal web series *The Guild*, which ran for six seasons and won numerous awards for web video excellence. She expanded the brand into numerous merchandising opportunities, including a hit comic book series with Dark Horse Comics. Costumes and props from the show are in the Smithsonian American History collection as examples of early web media pioneering.

In 2012 Felicia created a digital production company called Geek & Sundry. Since its launch, the channel has garnered more than two million subscribers on YouTube and spawned such hit series as *Tabletop* and *Critical Role*. In 2015, the company was sold to Legendary Entertainment. Felicia currently works on her own writing, acting, and producing projects. She streams video games on Twitch weekly and has a podcast called *Felicitations*. And while doing all that, she tries to be the best mother she can be.